Andrea Mantegna: Drawings in Close Up

By Roger Godfrey

First Editior

*****

I0474590

Andrea Mantegna: Drawings in Close Up
*****

Foreword

Andrea Mantegna (1431-1506), one of the foremost north Italian painters of the 15th century. A master of perspective and foreshortening, he made important contributions to the compositional techniques of Renaissance painting and drawing. Like other artists of the time, Mantegna experimented with perspective, e.g., by lowering the horizon in order to create a sense of greater monumentality. He also led a workshop that was the leading producer of prints in Venice before 1500.

Mantegna developed a passionate interest in classical antiquity. The influence of both ancient Roman sculpture and the contemporary sculptor Donatello are clearly evident in Mantegna's rendering of the human figure. His human forms were distinguished for their solidity, expressiveness, and anatomical correctness.

Trained as he had been in the study of marbles and the severity of the antique, Mantegna openly avowed that he considered ancient art superior to nature as being more eclectic in form. As a result, the painter exercised precision in outline, privileging the figure. Overall, Mantegna's work thus tended towards rigidity, demonstrating an austere wholeness rather than graceful sensitivity of expression.

His draperies are tight and closely folded, being studied from models draped in paper and woven fabrics gummed in place. His figures are slim, muscular and bony; the action impetuous but of arrested energy. Finally, tawny landscape, gritty with littering pebbles, marks the athletic hauteur of his style.

Mantegna's later works varied in quality. His largest undertaking, a fresco series on the Triumphs of Caesar (1489), displays a rather dry classicism, but Parnassus (1497), an allegorical painting commissioned by Isabelle d'Este, is his freshest, most animated work. His work never ceased to be innovative. In Madonna of Victory (1495), he introduced a new compositional arrangement, based on diagonals, which was later to be exploited by Correggio, while his Dead Christ was a tour de force of foreshortening that pointed ahead to the style of 16th-century Mannerism.

One of the key artistic figures of the second half of the 15th century, Mantegna was the dominant influence on north Italian art for 50 years. It was also through him that German artists, notably Albrecht Durer, were made aware of the artistic discoveries of the Italian Renaissance.

Drawings

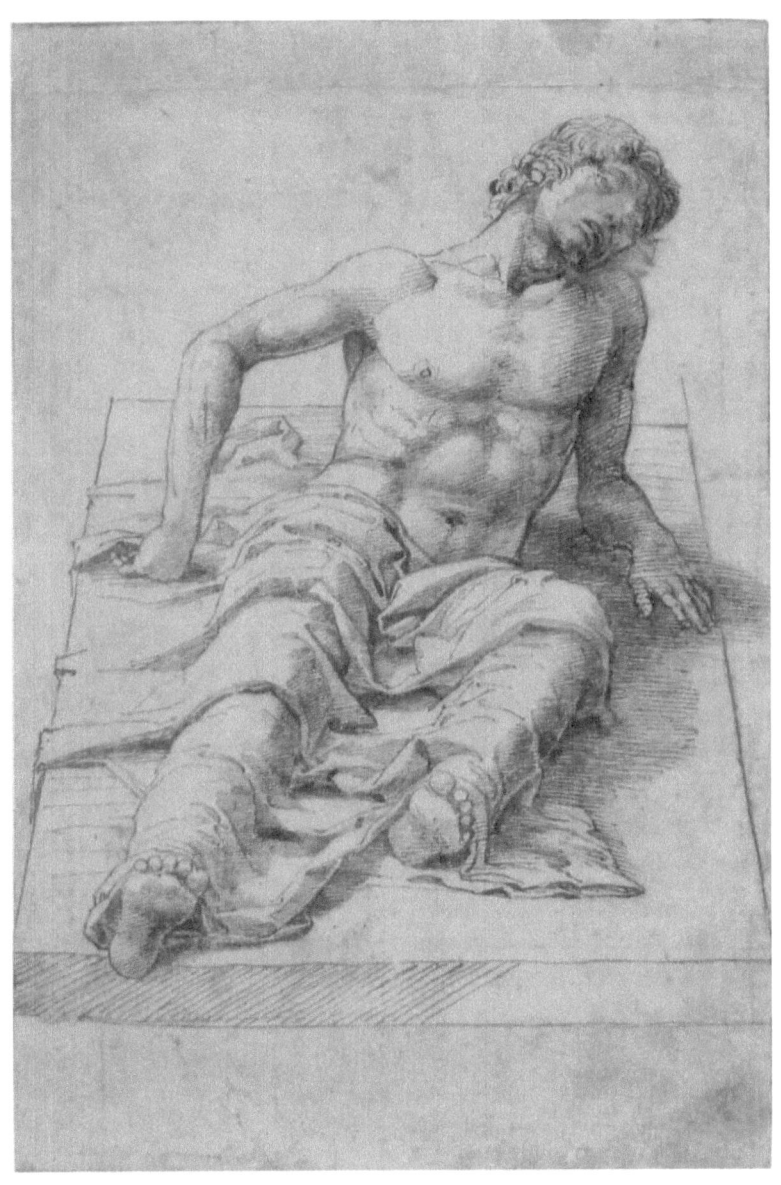

Study for a Christ, 1478-1490, pen and ink

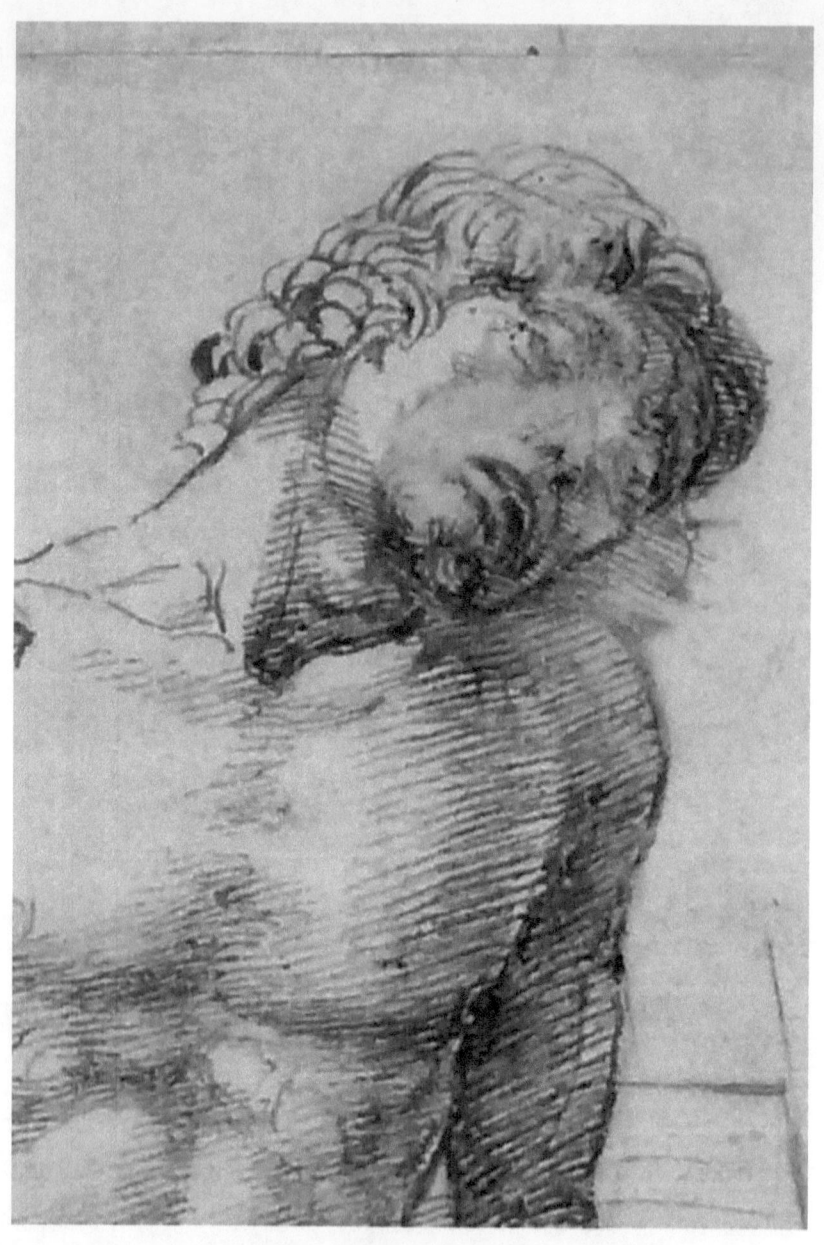

Detail

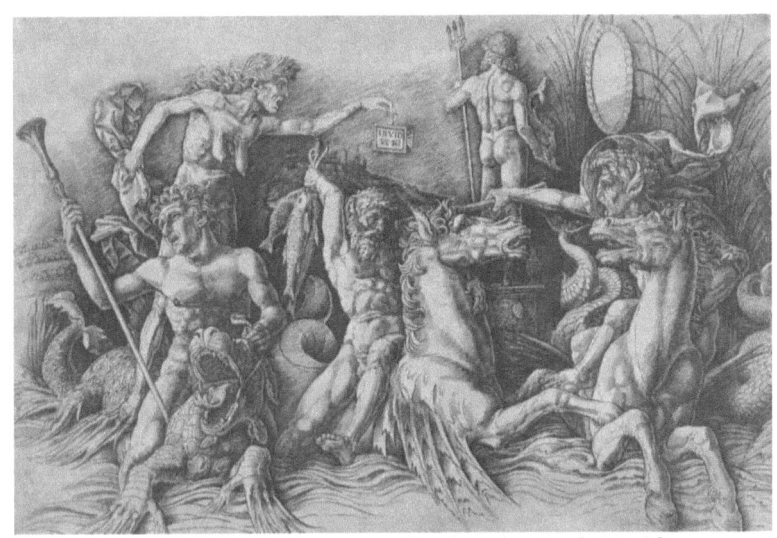

The Battle of the Sea Gods (the Left Half)
1475, Engraving and drypoint

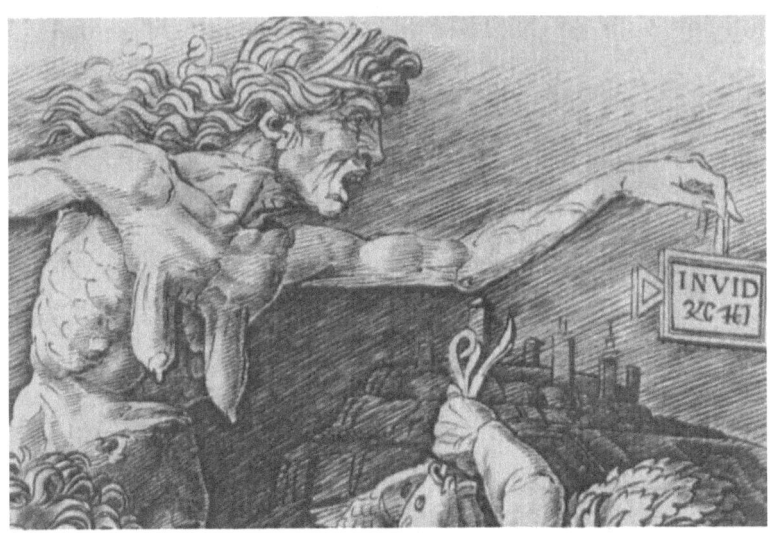

Detail

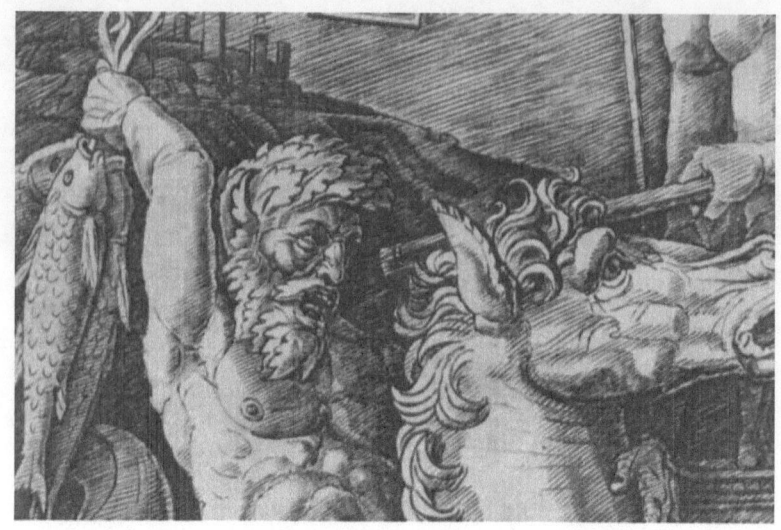

The word "INVID", which is inscribed on the plate the old woman with a terrifying look is holding, is an abbreviation of INVIDIA, the Latin word for "jealousy".

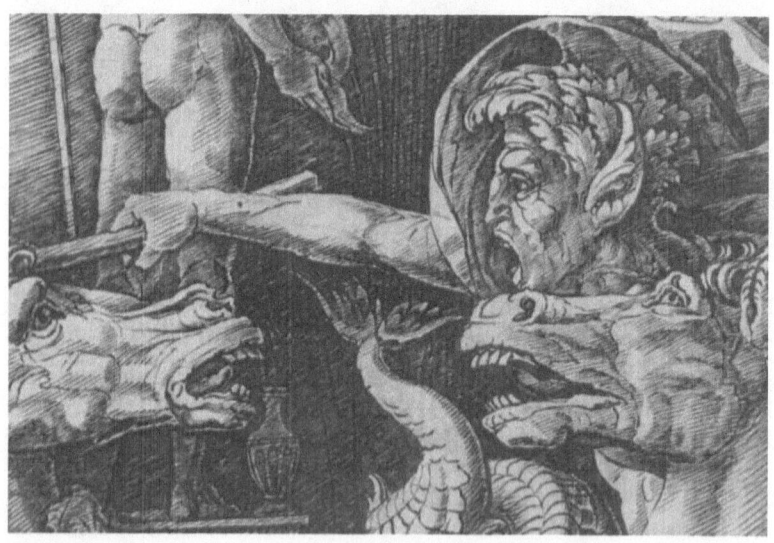

Detail

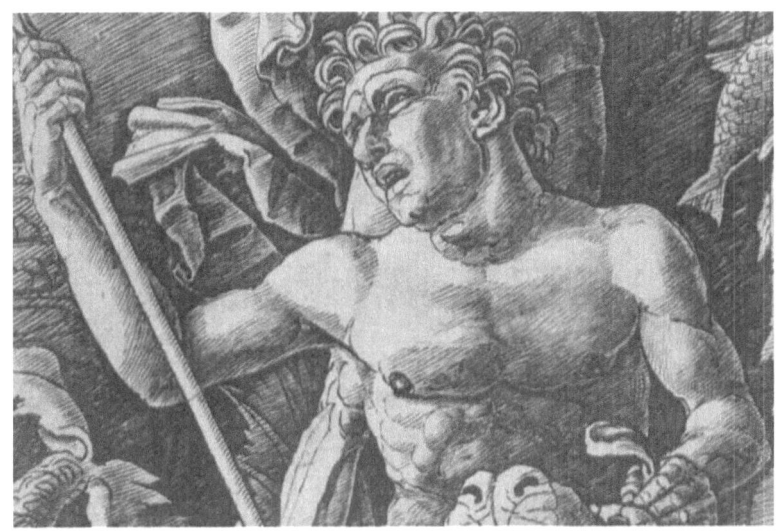

Detail

Regarding the interpretation of the theme of this mysterious print, some say it has to do with ichthyophagists referred to in "Bibiliotheca historica" by the ancient Greek historian Diodorus while others identify general literature of the time including Strabo's "Geography" as the source. This print is the left half of an oblong composition of a sequential frieze.

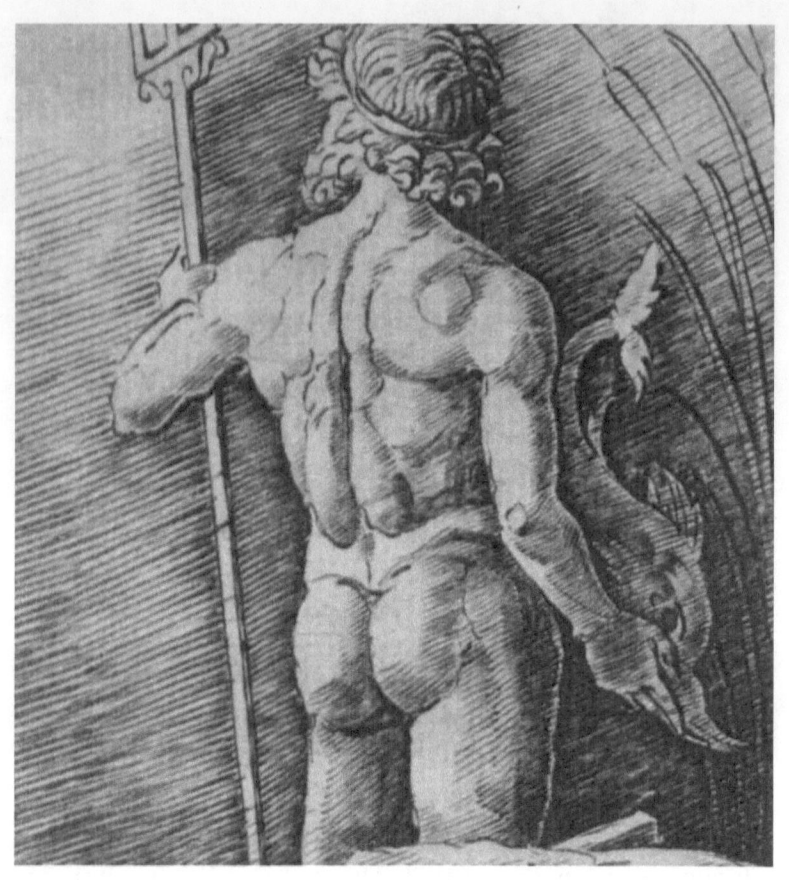

Detail

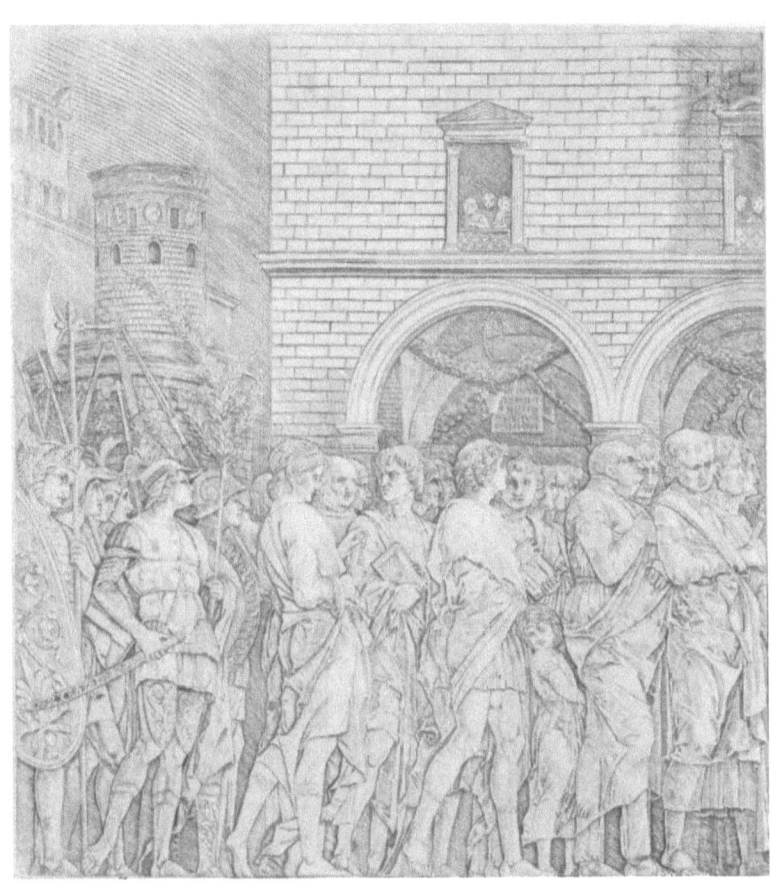

Triumph of Senators
Undated, Ink on paper

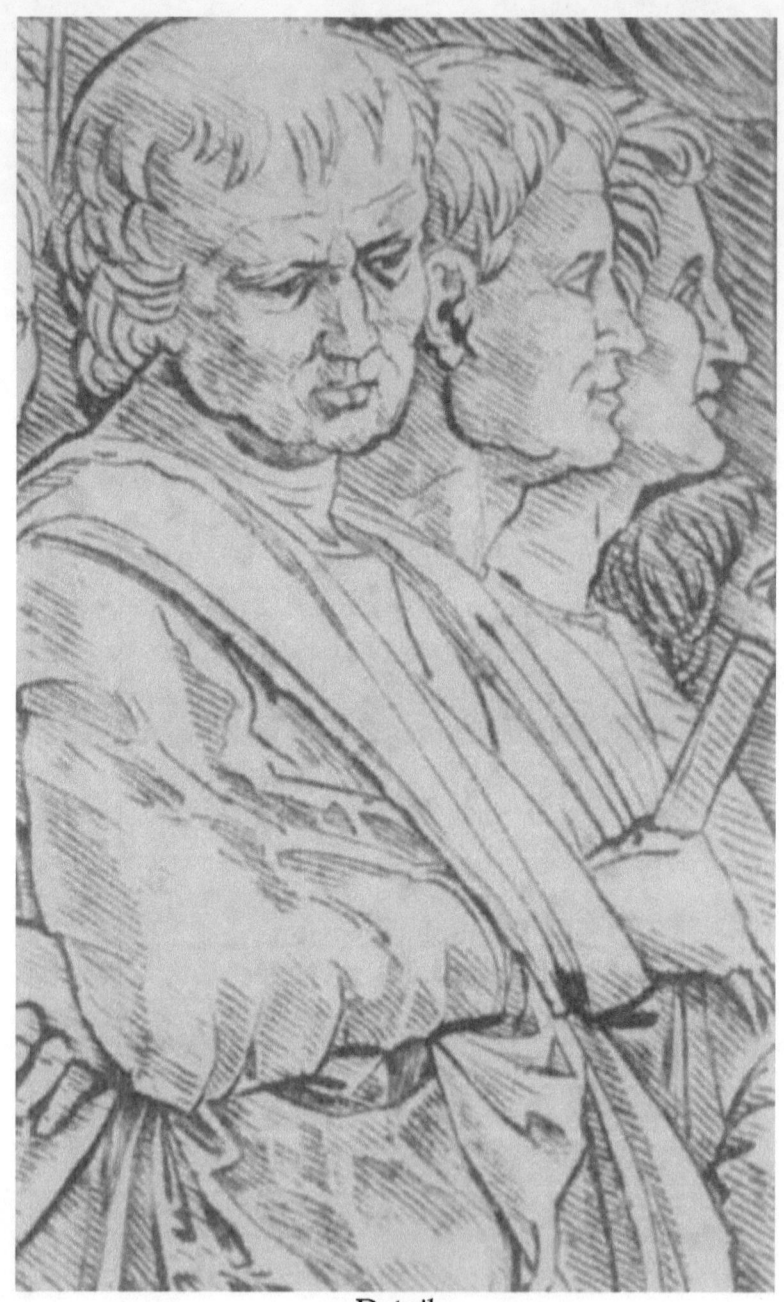

Detail

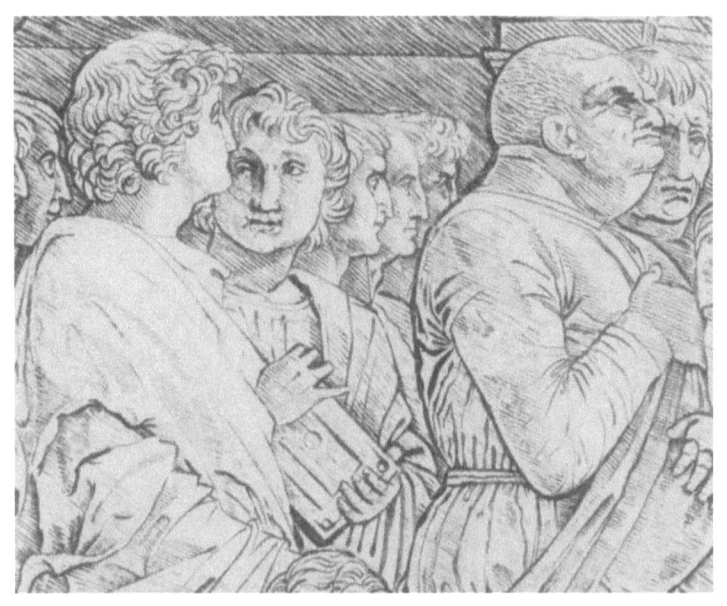

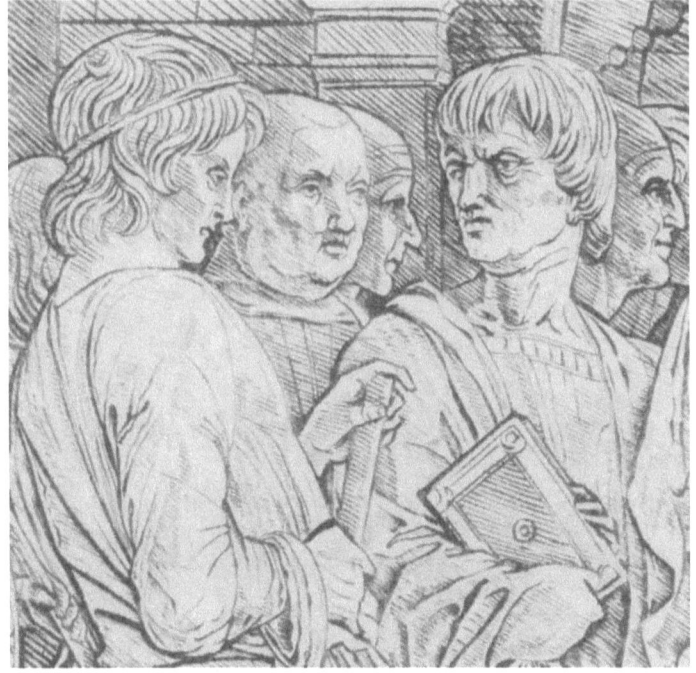

Details

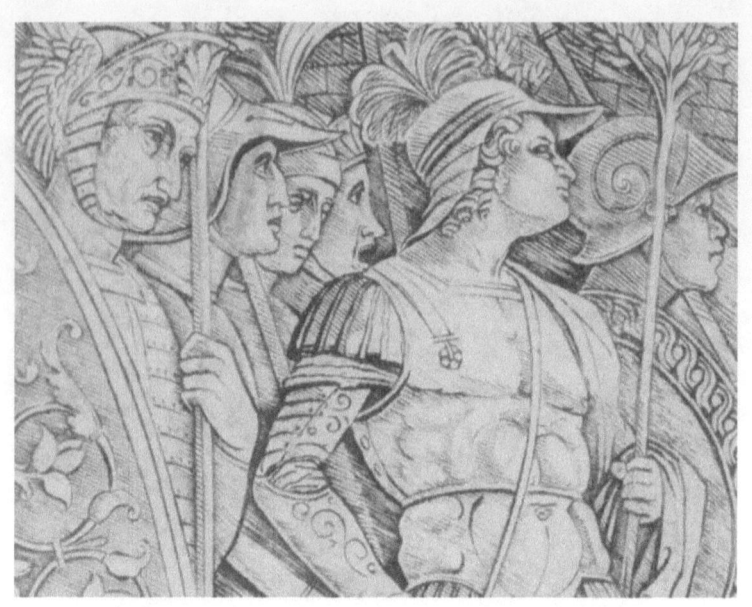

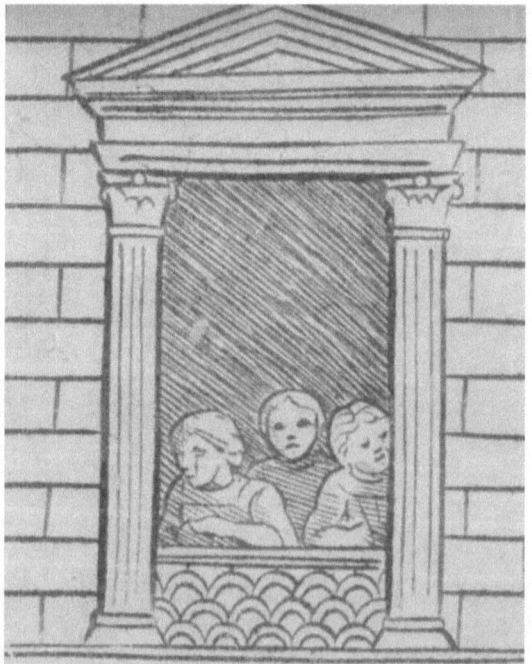

Details

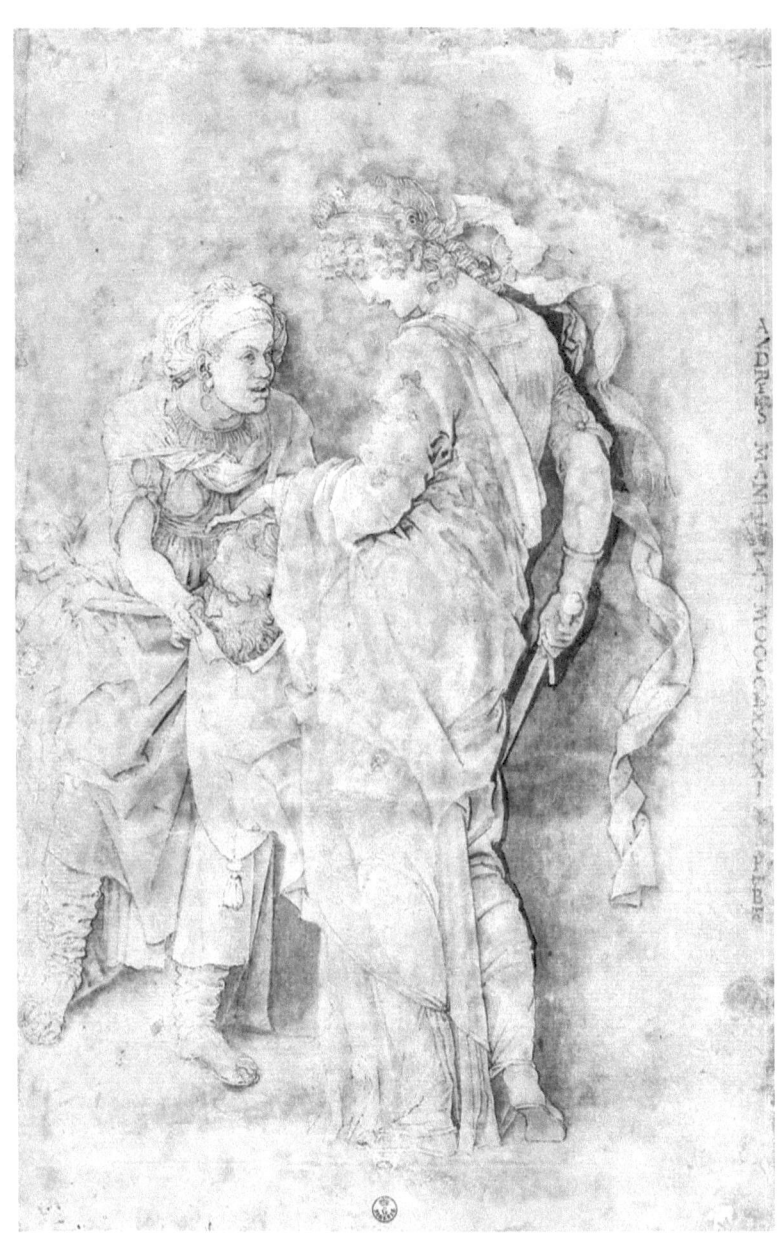

Judith with the Head of Holofernes
1490-95

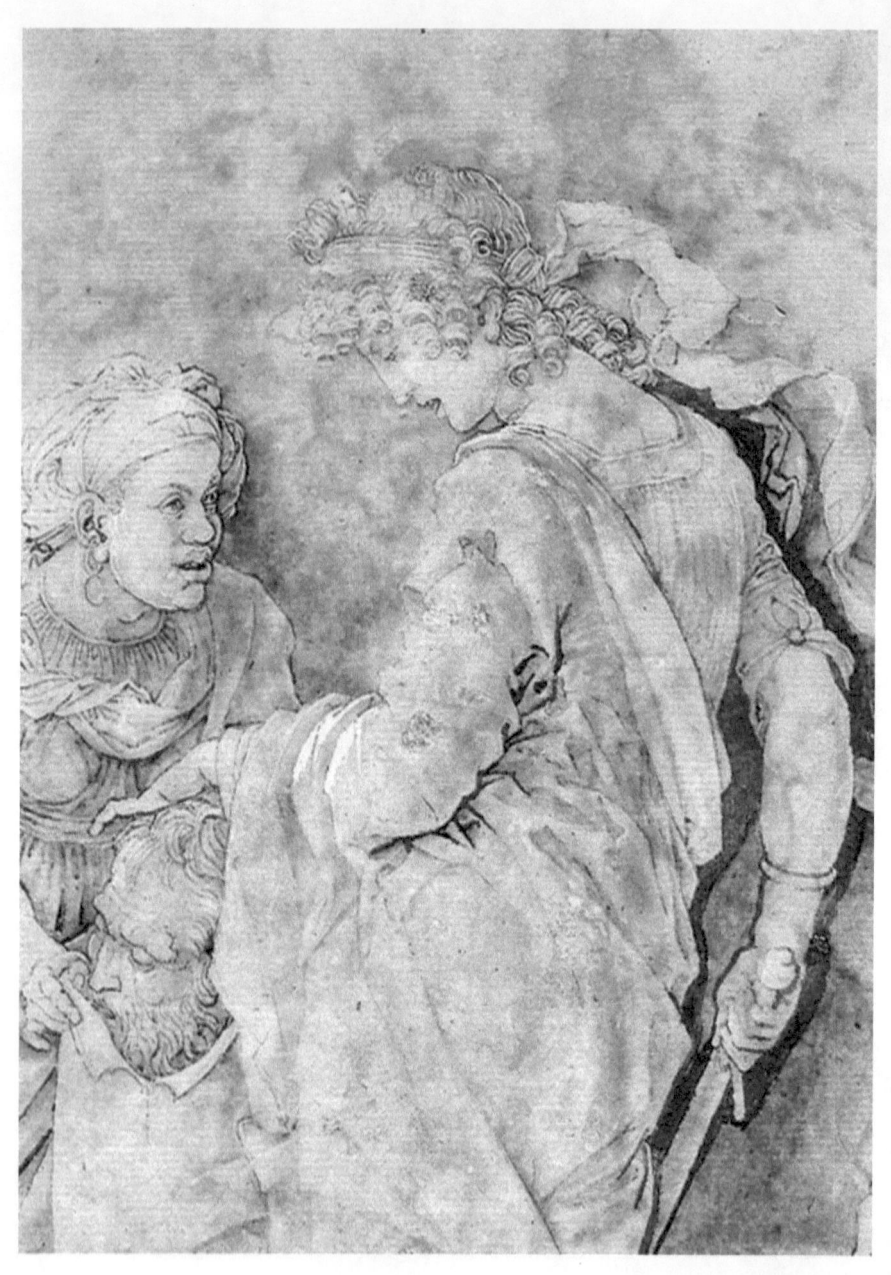

Detail

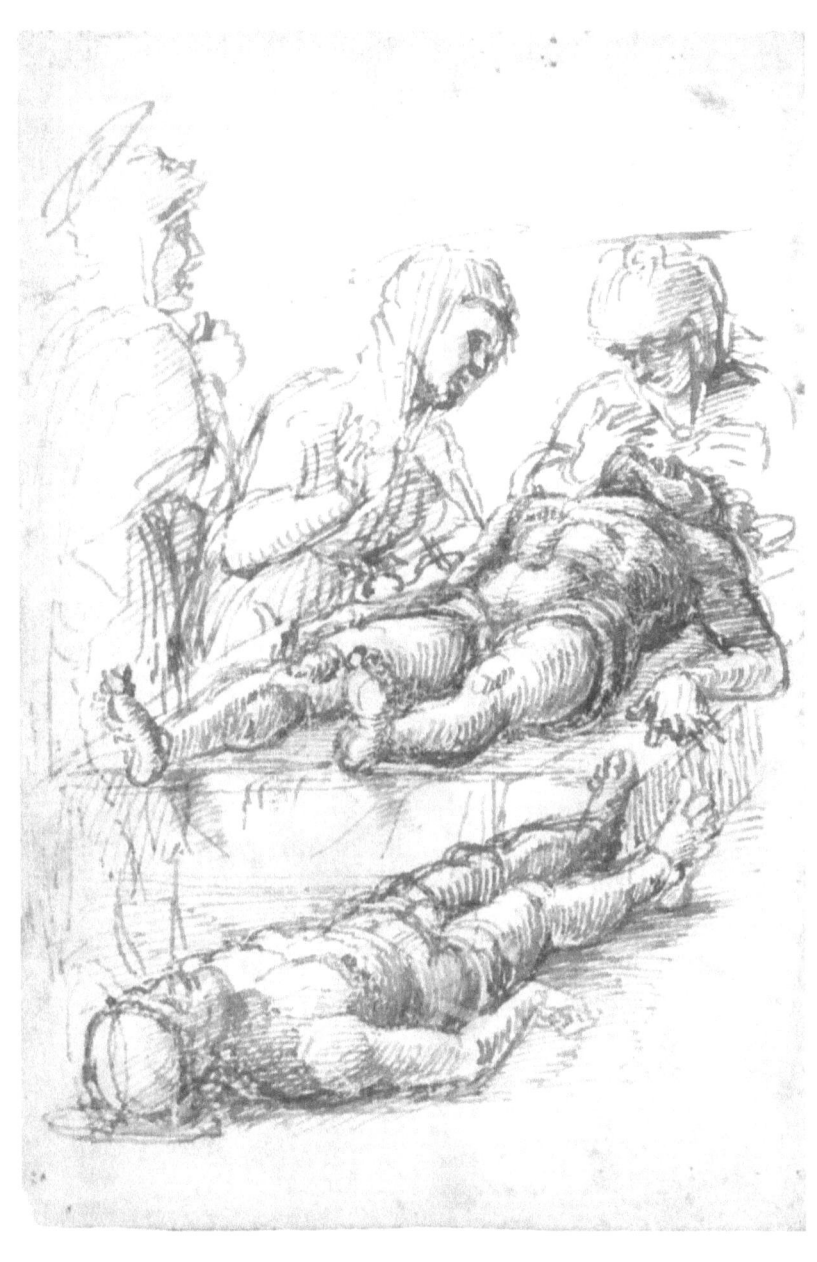

Lamentation of the Christ (Study for Pieta -recto)
1460, ink

The body of Jesus lies on a marble bier while his mother Mary, Mary Magdalene and St. John the Apostle mourn over him. On the ground in front of the slab is another view of the dead Christ, this one lying in the opposite direction with his head closest to the viewer. On the back (verso) of the page is a *Pietà*, Mary cradling the body of her crucified son, holding his wrist almost as if she were checking for a pulse.

These drawings are very reminiscent of *Lamentation over the Dead Christ*, now in the Pinacoteca di Brera in Milan, which uses extreme perspective to emphasize Christ's suffering and humanity. The figure of Christ is shockingly foreshortened, with his pierced feet in foreground, his pierced hands posed vertically so the ragged nail holes are in the viewer's direct line of sight. His mother Mary, her face deeply lined with age, weeps beside him, but you can only see her face and hand. In front of her is St. John and he's even more cropped with just a sliver of his face and a bit of his clasped hands visible. Behind Mary you can barely glimpse the mouth of another woman opened as if wailing in grief. This is Mary Magdalene, specifically identified by the presence of the unguent jar on the right back of Christ's funerary slab.

The body of Christ in newly discovered drawings, while not as extremely positioned, is angled backwards. Mantegna is playing with perspective in the recto, flipping the body around to see how it looks with the head in front. Notice also the hands, that quasi-verticle awkward angle which props the palms up on the fingers so the stigmata can be clearly seen.

We don't know when exactly Mantegna painted *Lamentation over the Dead Christ* but it was probably in the 1480s. The pen and ink studies date to around 1460, so they are considerably older and thus were probably not preparatory for the later masterpiece. They do illustrate the artist's longstanding exploration of the subject, however.

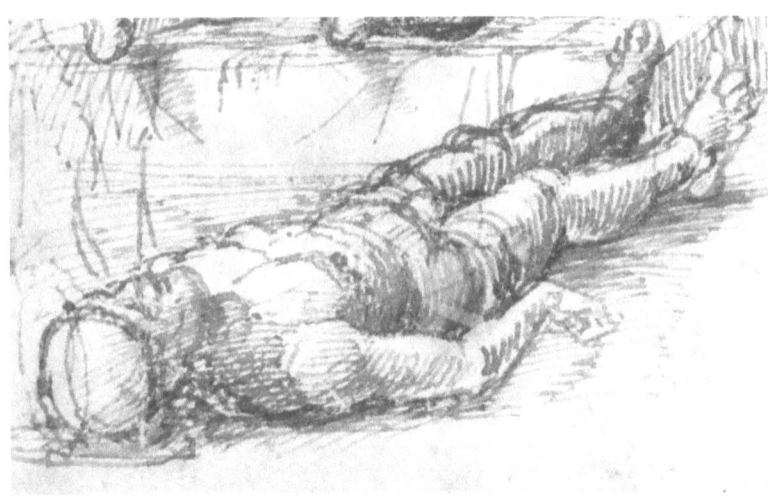

Detail

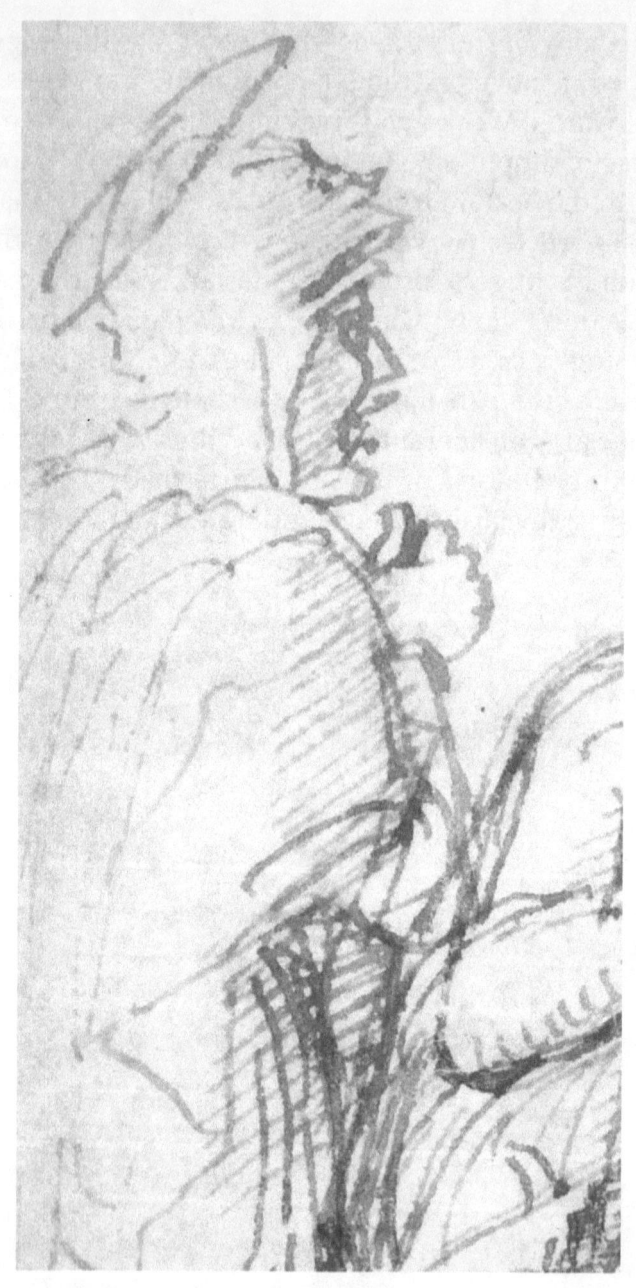

Detail

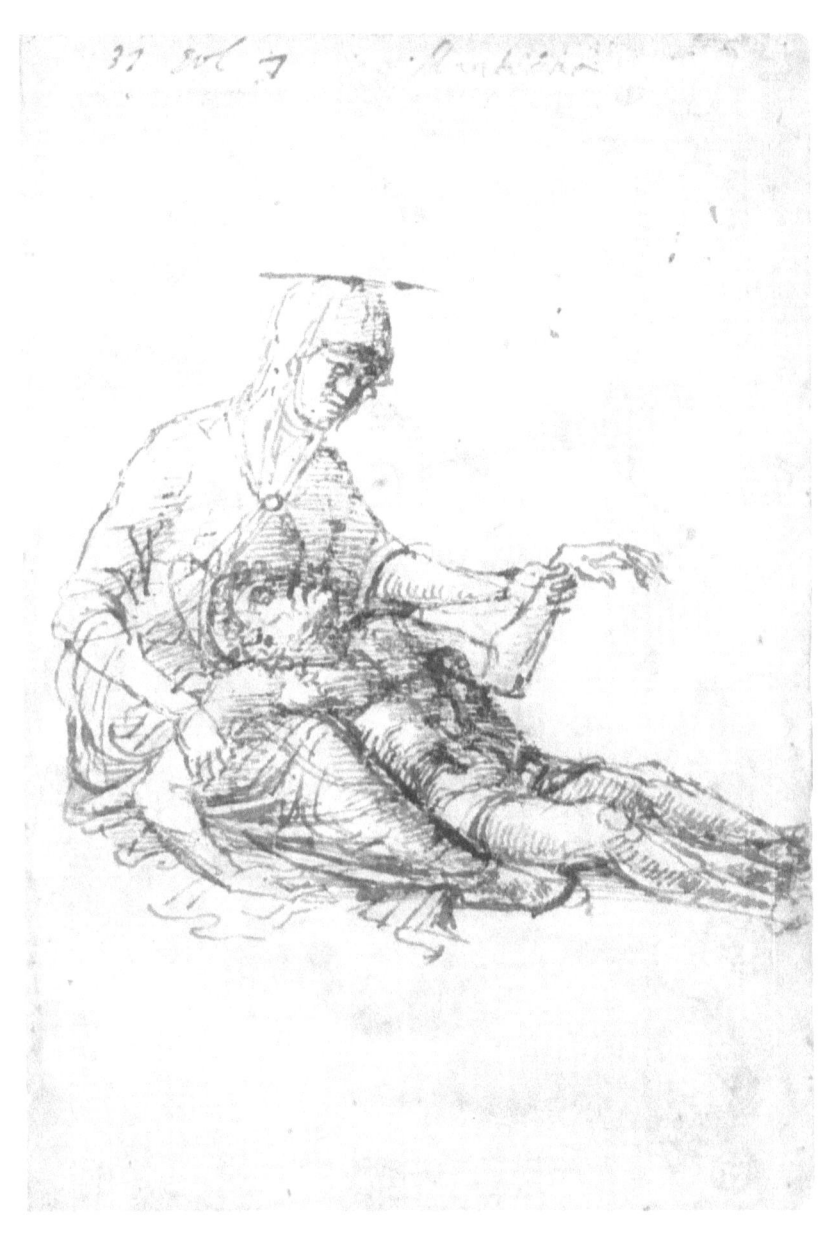

Lamentation of the Christ (Study for Pieta -verso)
1460, ink

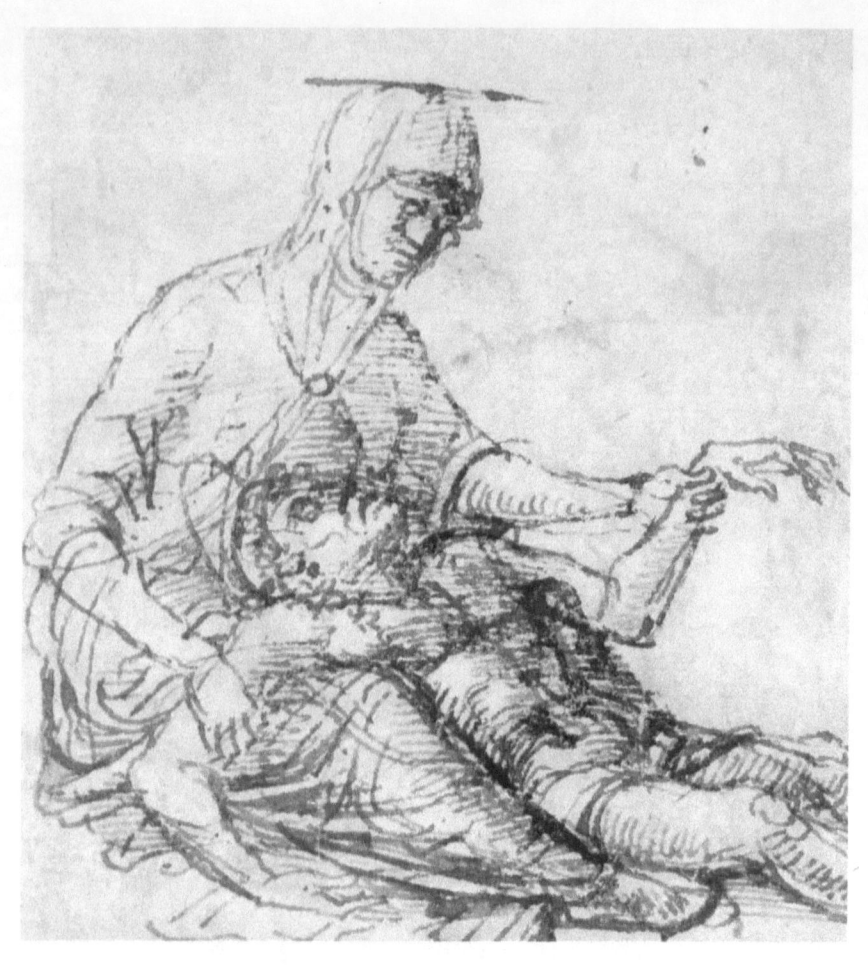

Detail

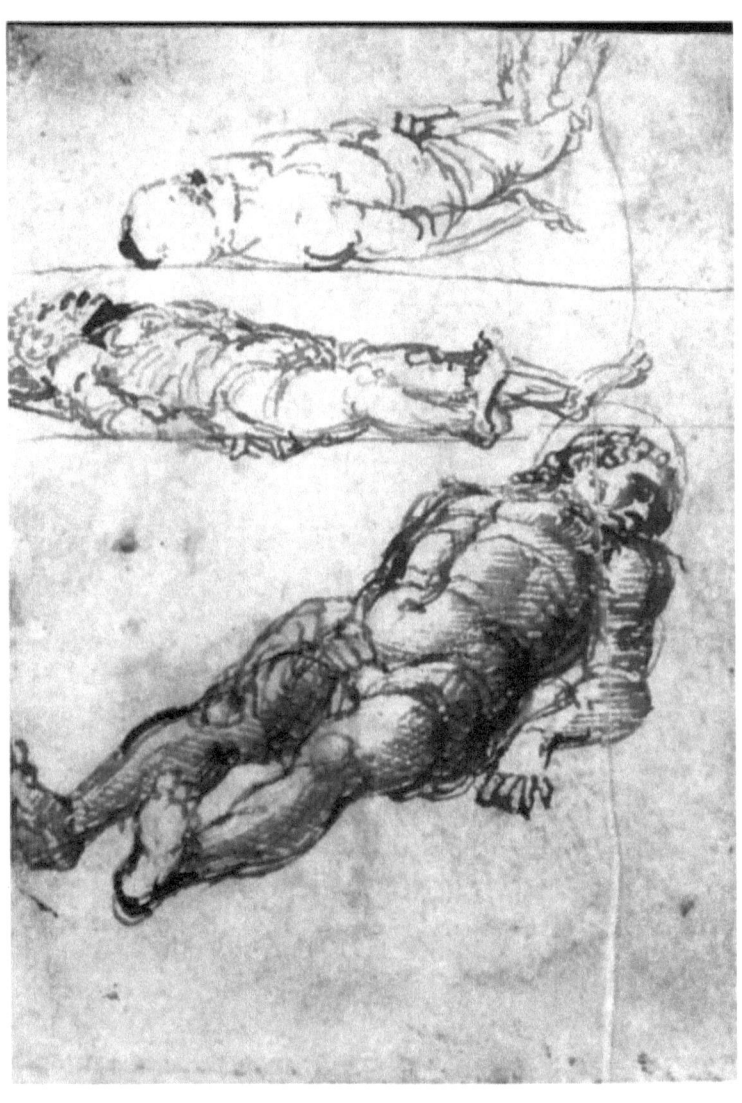

Three studies elongated figures, 1455, pen and ink

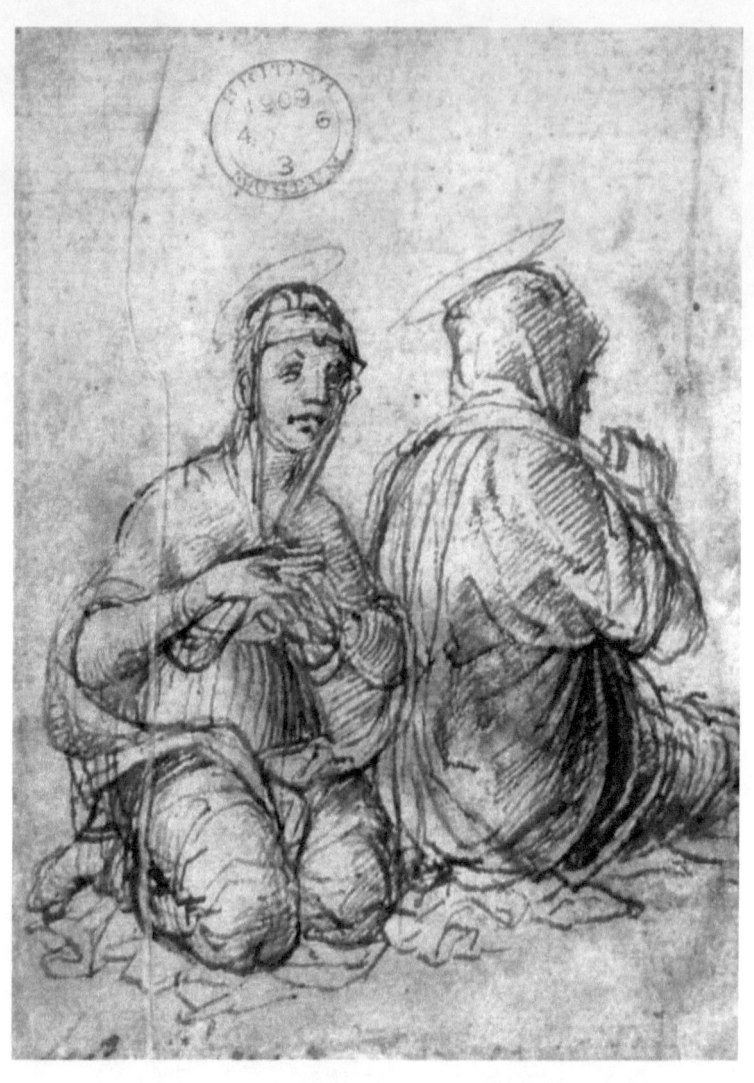

Two holy women in prayer, 1455, pen and ink

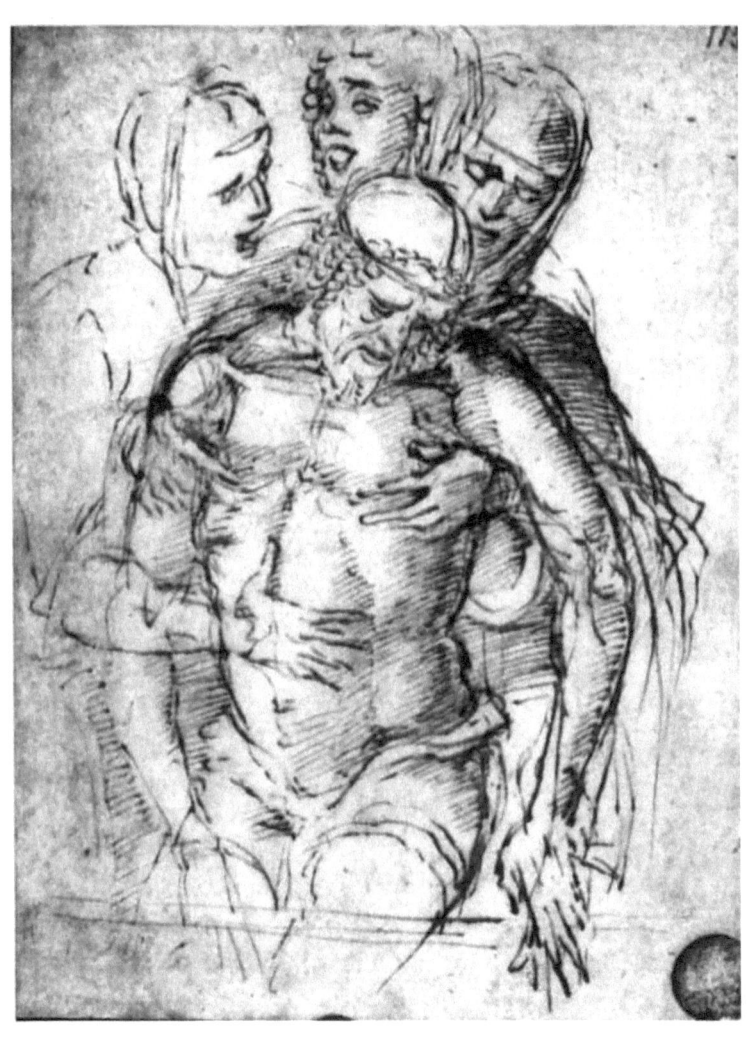

Pieta, 1459, pen and ink

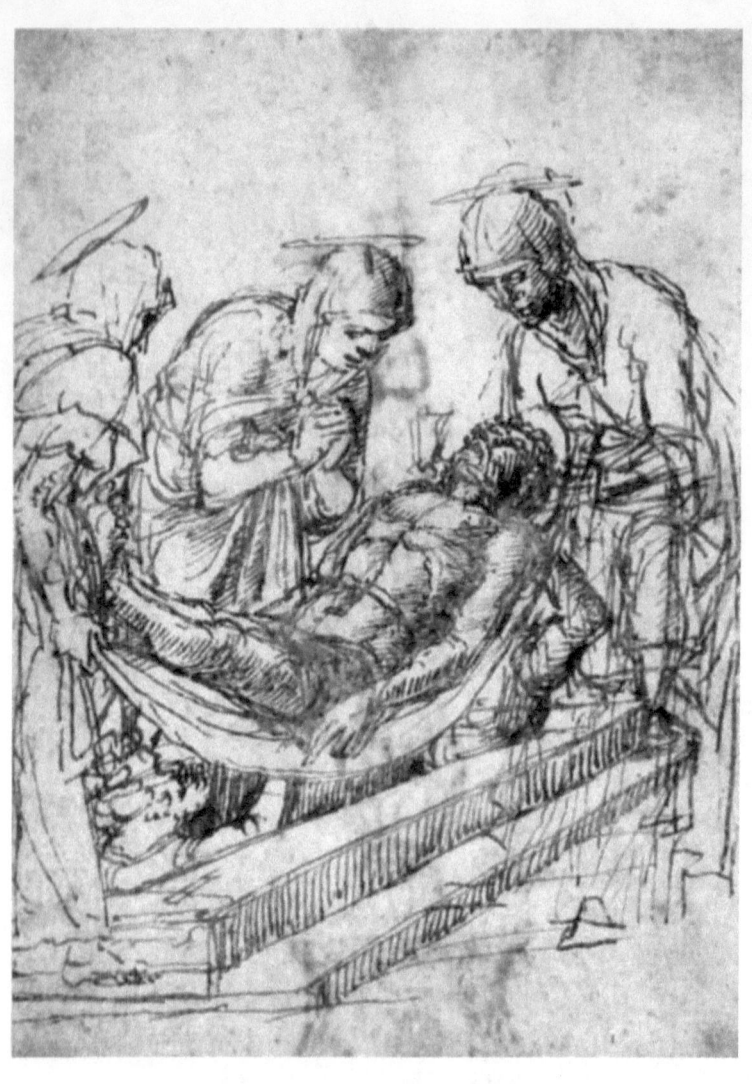

The Entombment, 1459, pen and ink

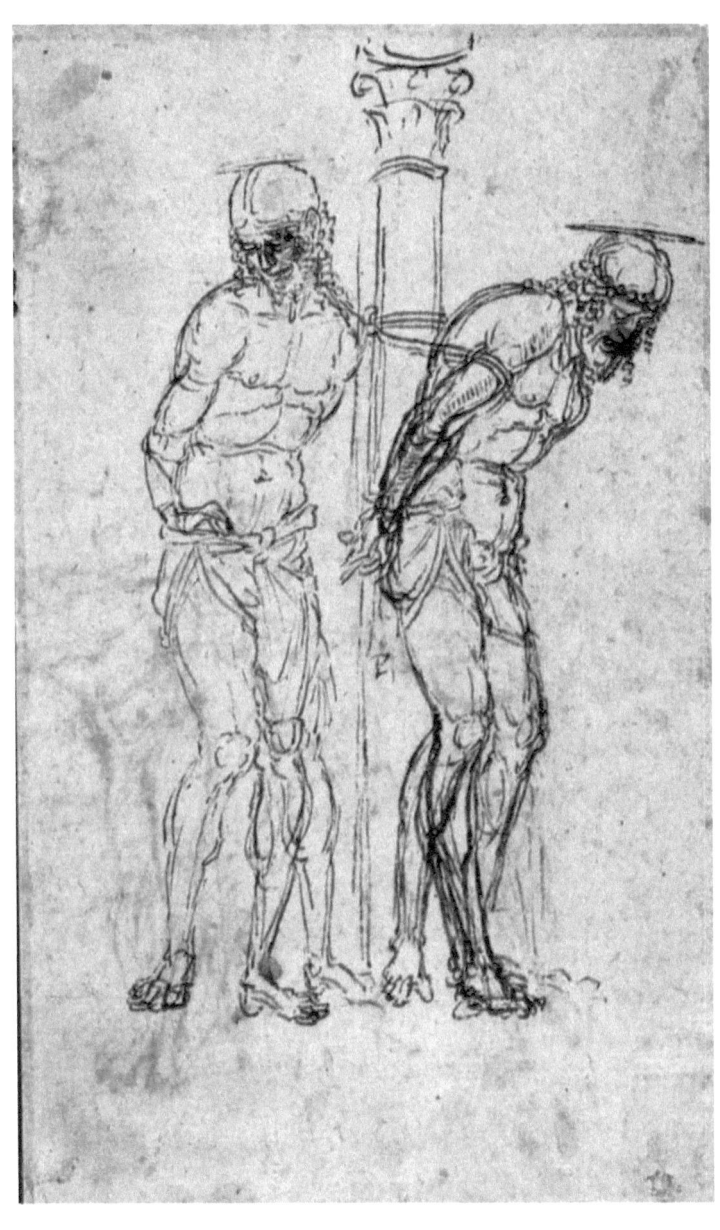

Two Studies for Christ at the Column, 1459, pen and ink

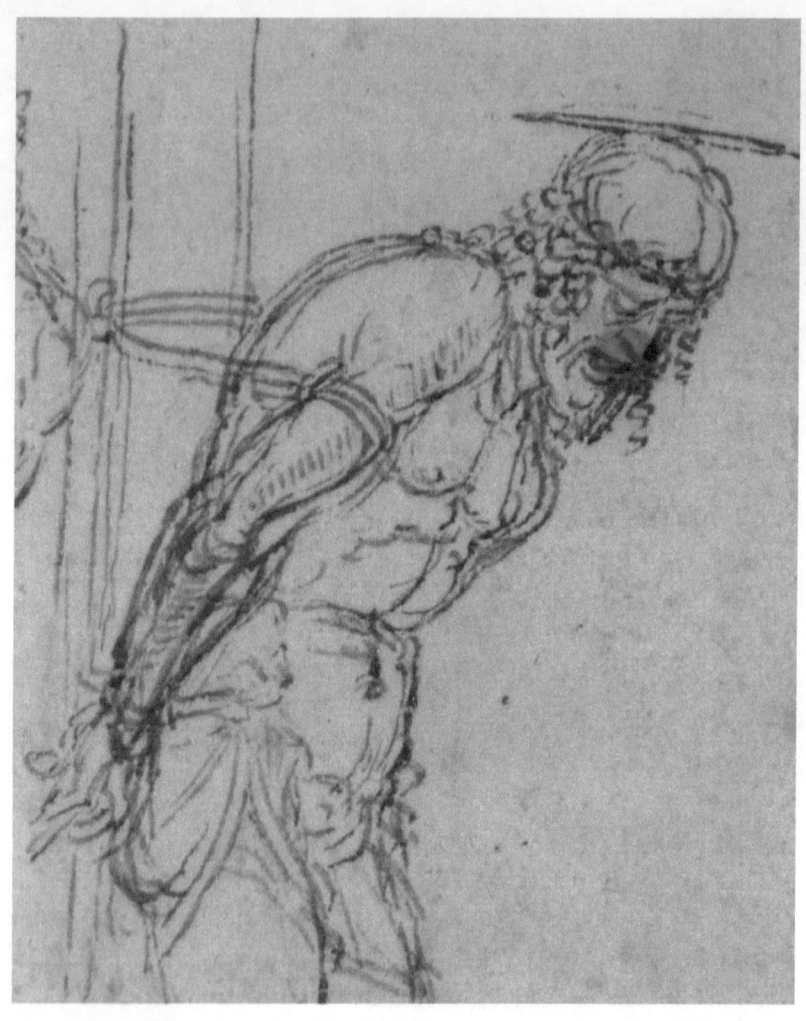

Here we see a heroic, idealized depiction of Christ, whose strong, muscular body contrasts with his down-turned head and facial agony. Mantegna was an ardent student of Greek and Roman sculpture and departing from the usual biblical account, he endows the Savior with a body worthy of a Greek God, while his head is bent and his facial expression, tormented and anguished.

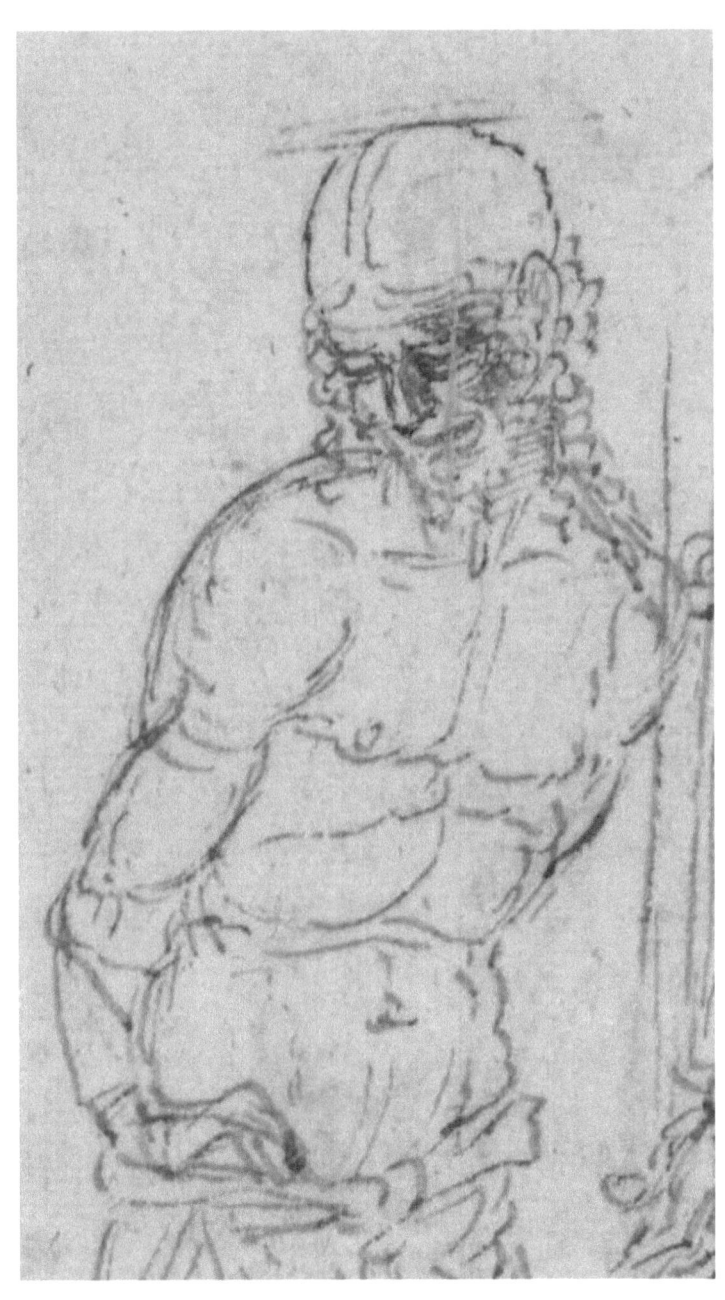

Detail

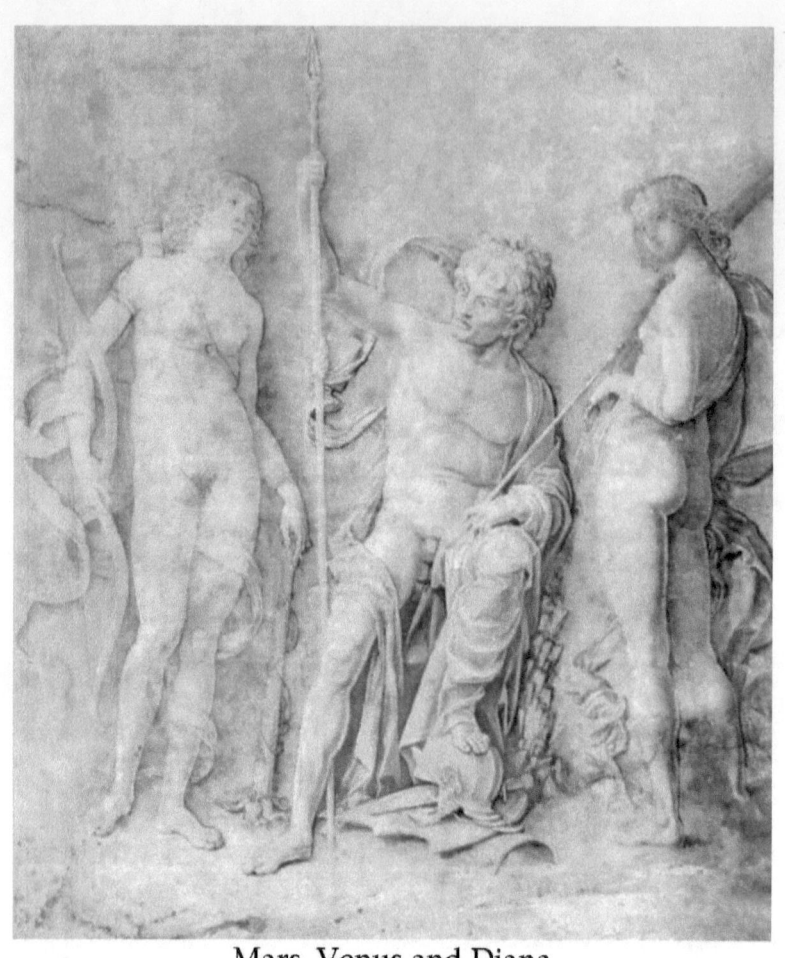

Mars, Venus and Diana
Undated

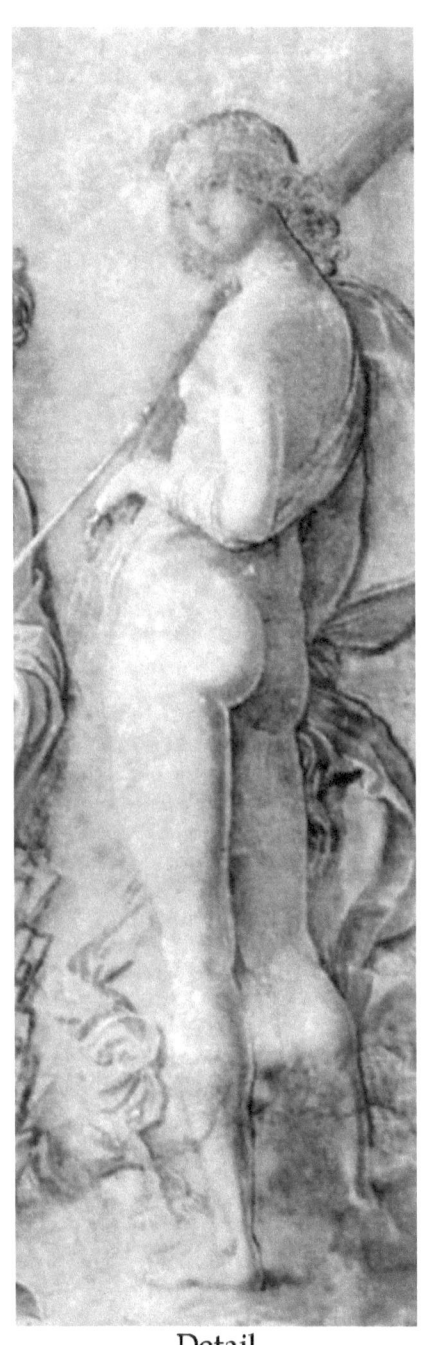

Detail

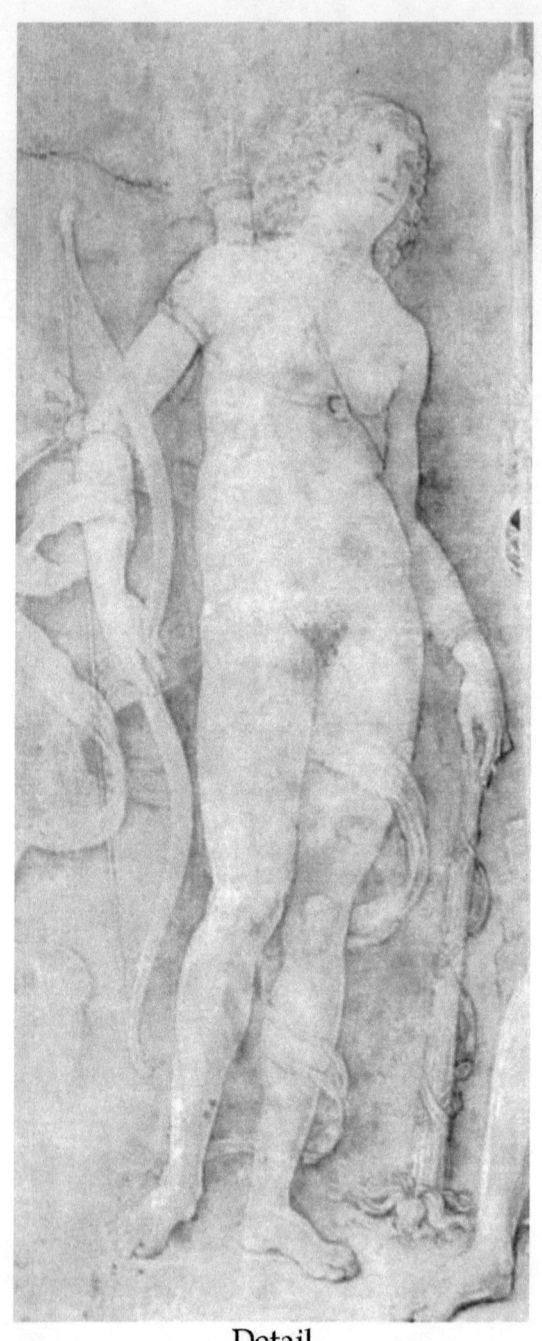

Detail

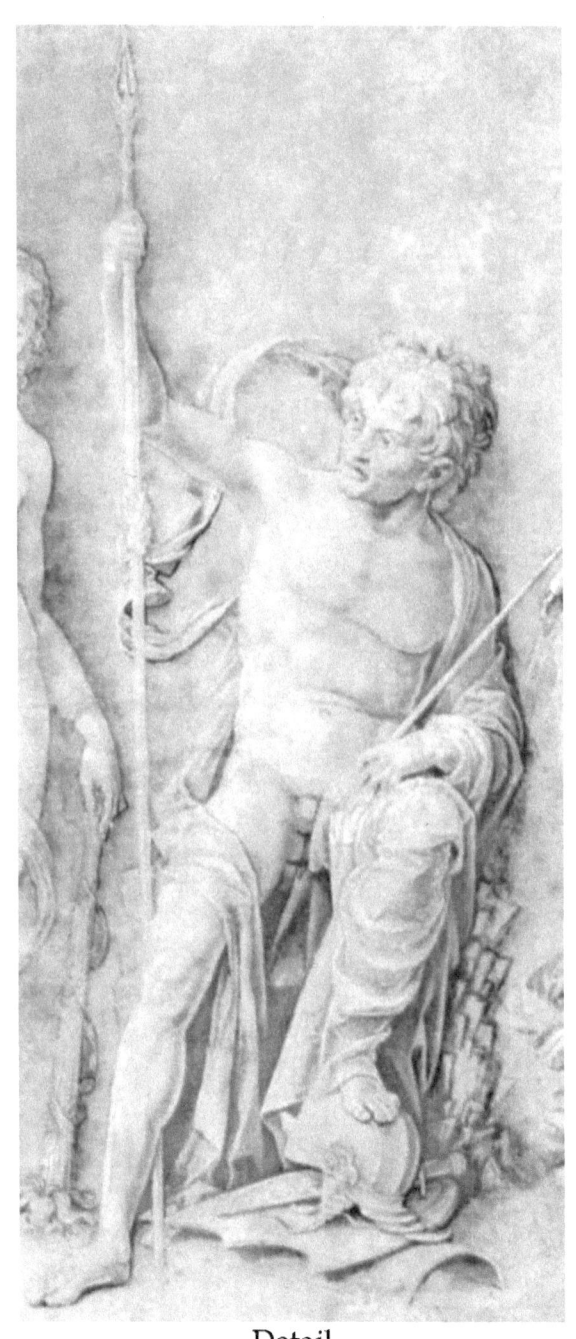

Detail

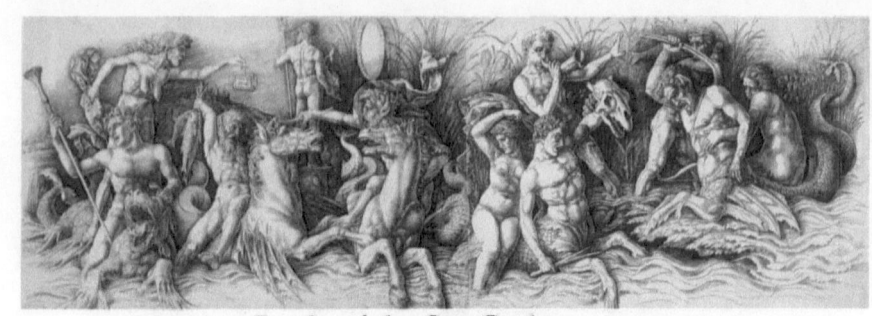

Battle of the Sea Gods
1470s, Engraving and drypoint, 283 x 826 mm

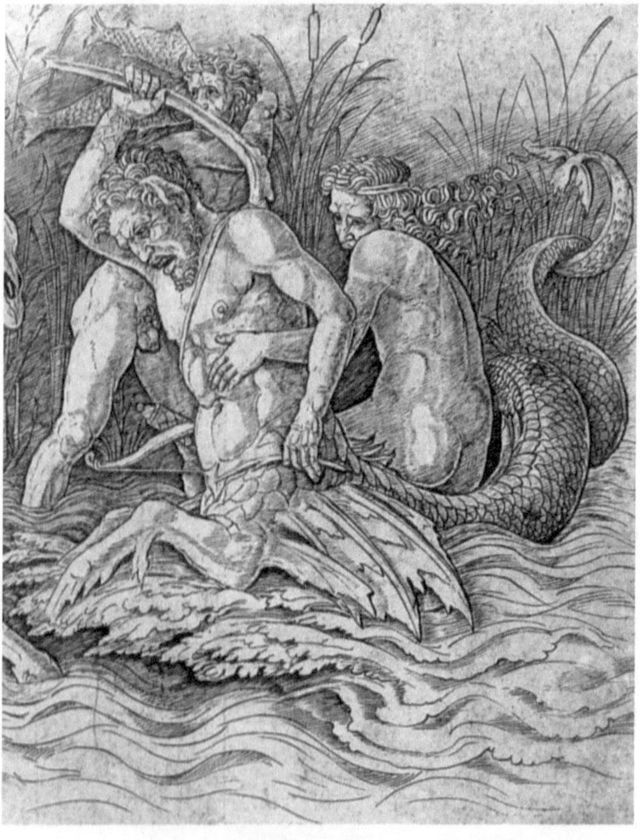

Detail

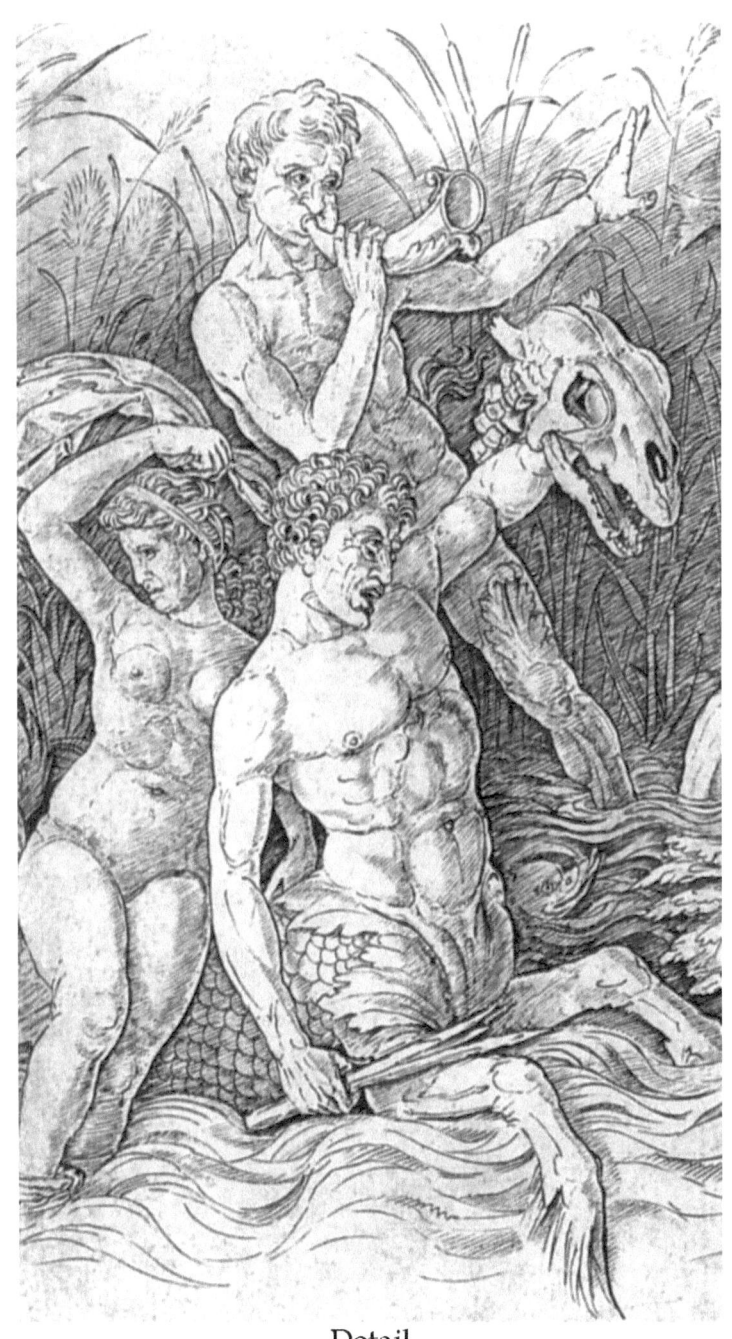

Detail

The print is made from two plates, printed on separate sheets of paper and joined at the centre. The print is an exercise in wit, the powerful, classical sea gods do battle with bones and knots of fish, hardly capable of defending them, while a standing statue of Neptune, the god of the sea, turns his back on the whole scene.

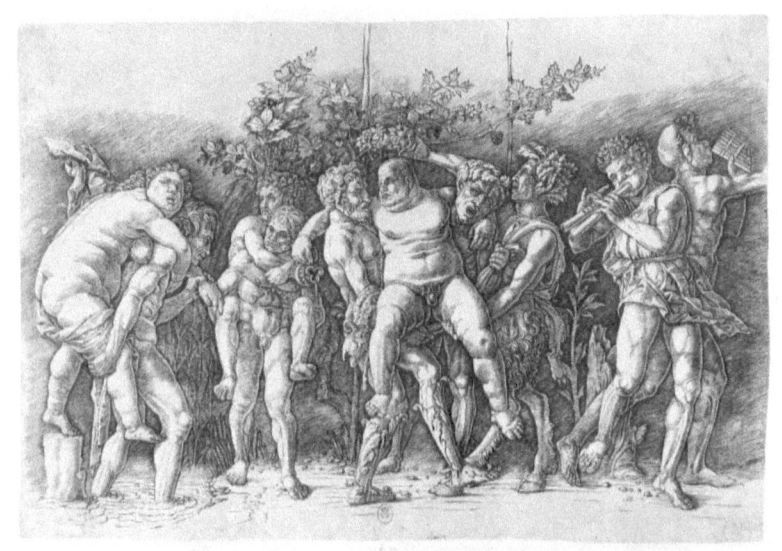

Bacchanal in Silene, 1480, Engraving

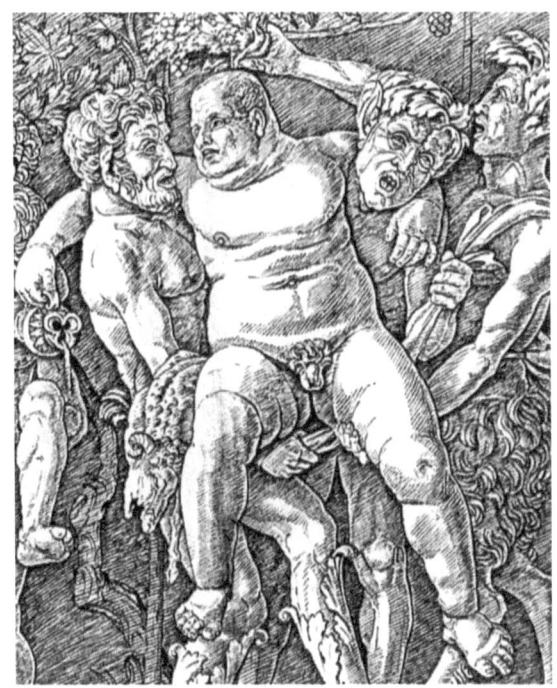

Detail

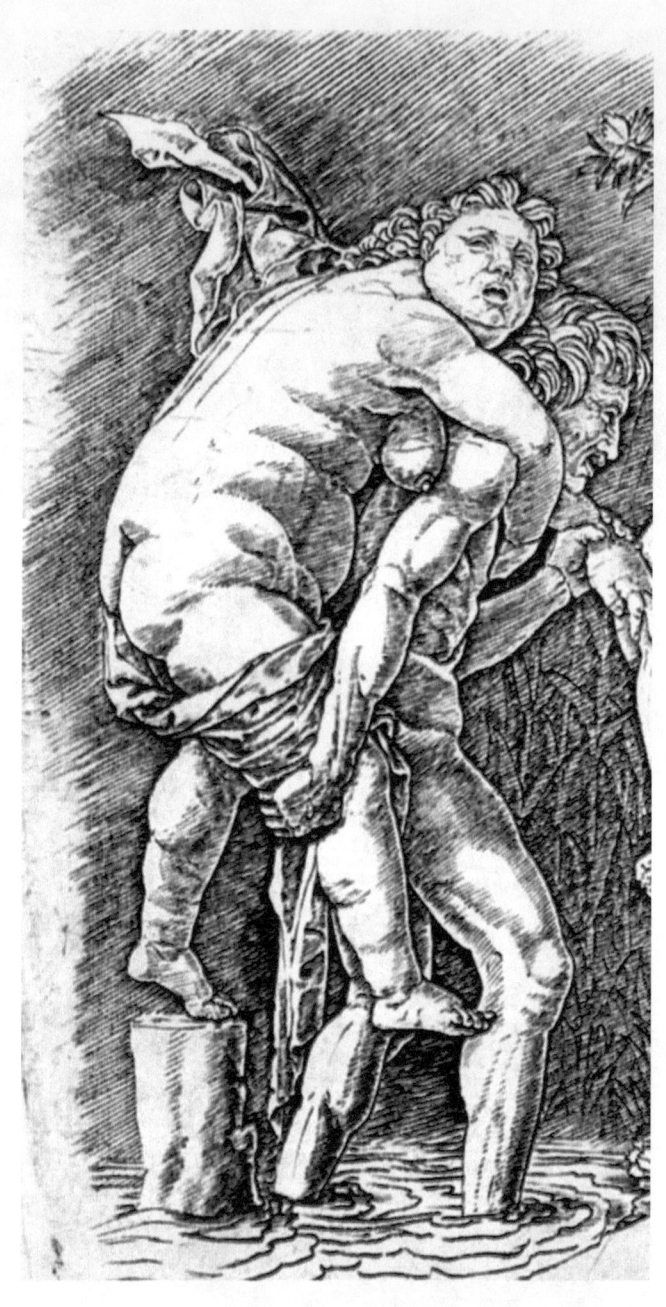

Detail

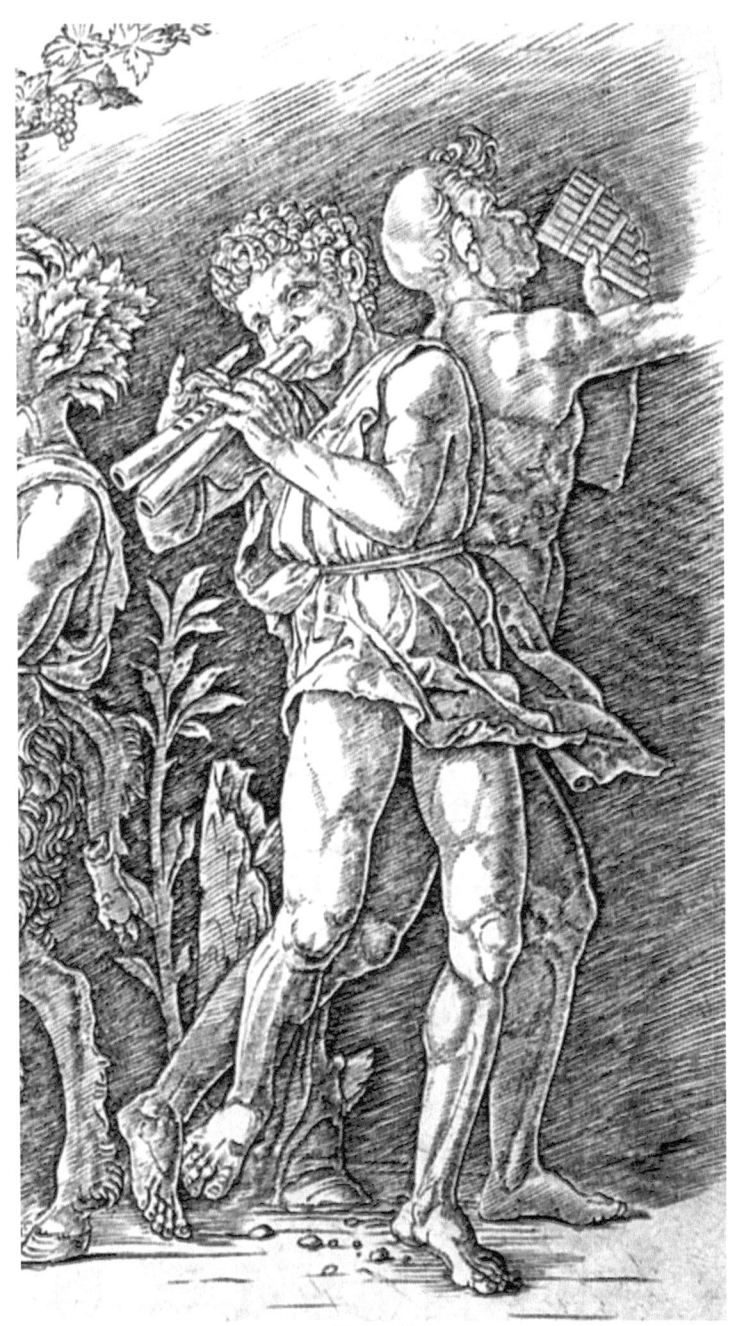

Detail

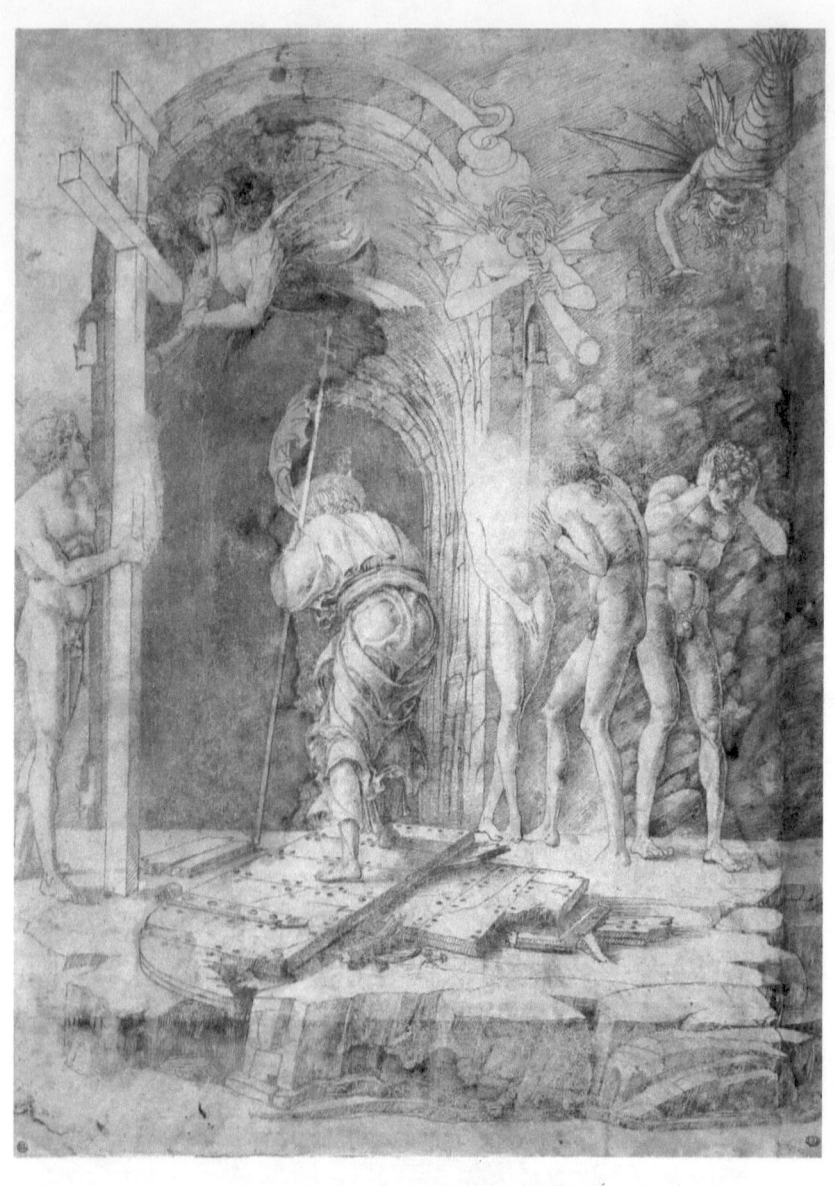

The Descent into Limbo
1468, Pen, brown ink and watercolor on vellum

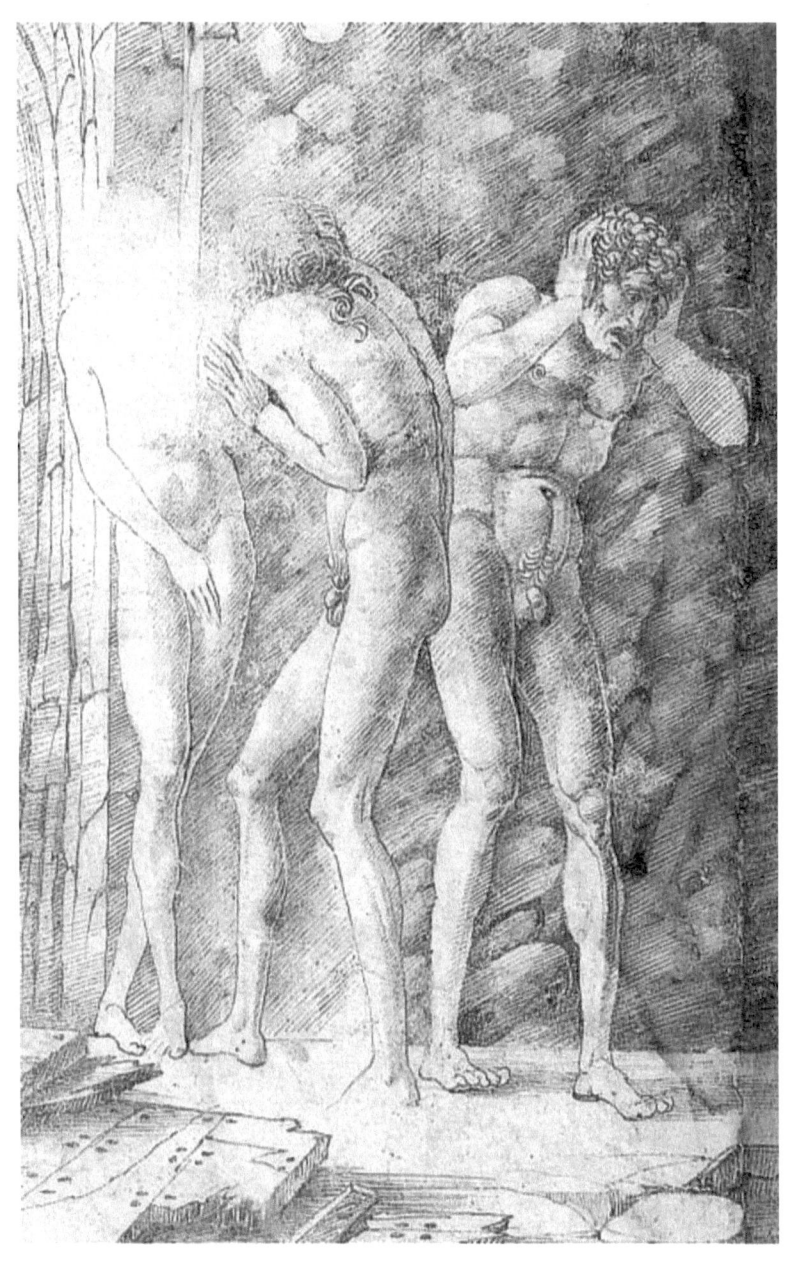

Detail

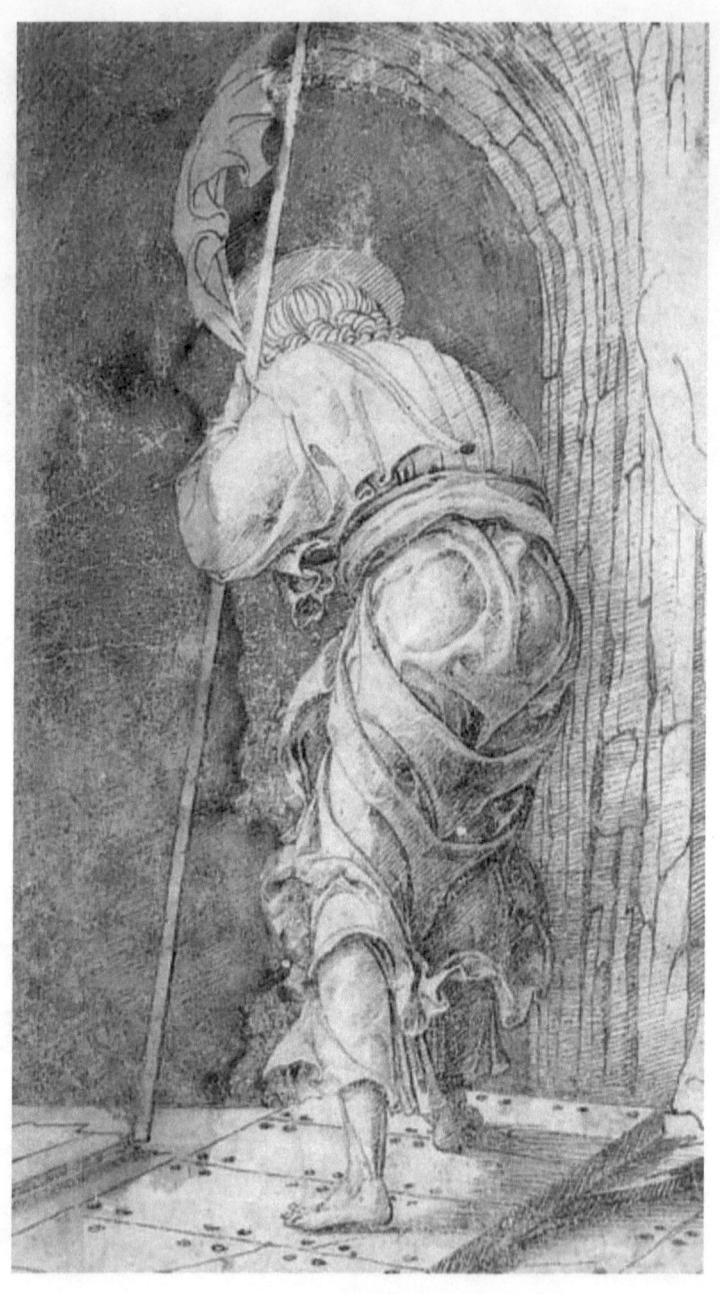

Detail

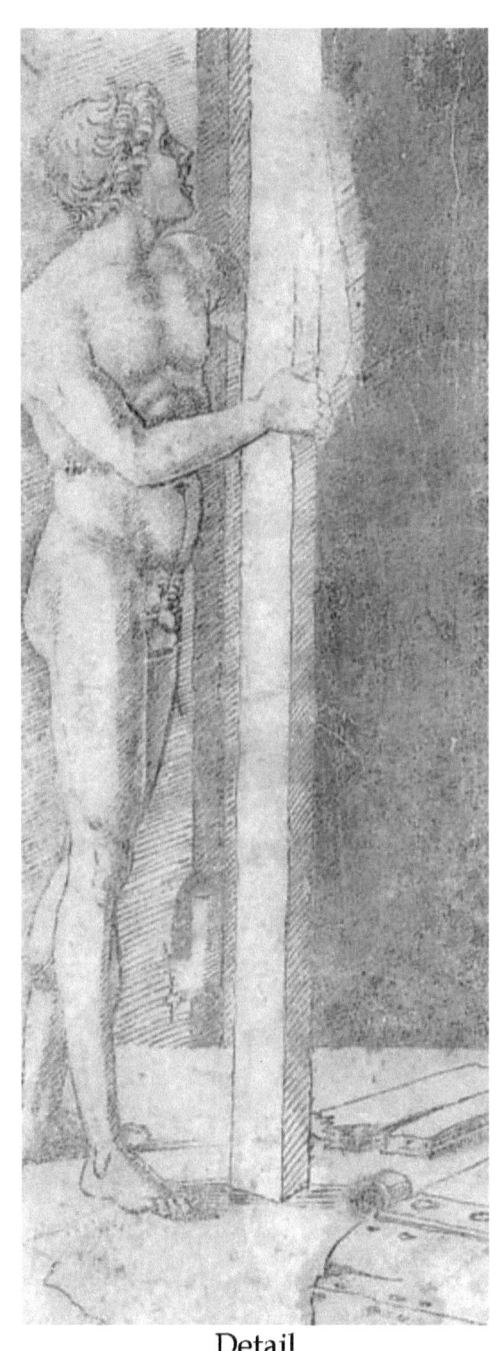

Detail

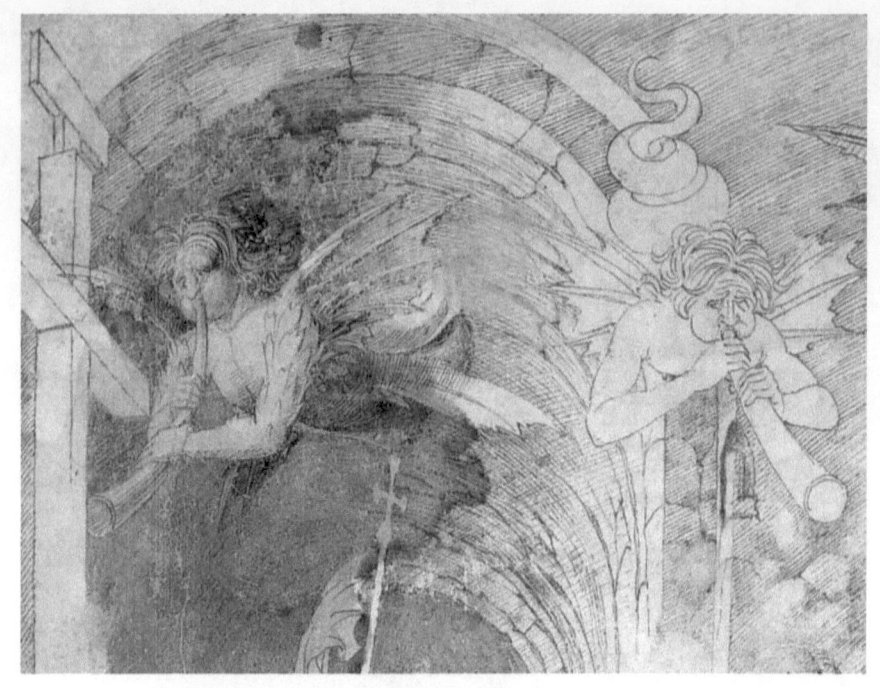

Detail

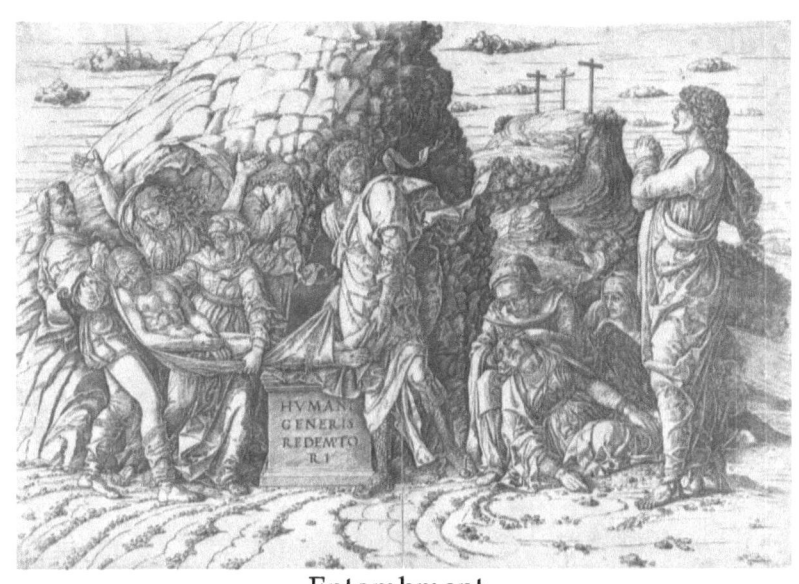

Entombment
1470-1475, Burin and dry point; H. 29.9 cm; W. 44.2 cm

In 1550, in his "Life" of the artist, Giorgio Vasari described Mantegna as the inventor of copperplate engraving in Italy, thus creating a real myth. Specialists are still divided over this question: some consider that Mantegna never handled a burin himself but provided designs for printmaking. As court painter, Mantegna was under the strict control of the Gonzaga family who forbade him to sell his works. This new reproduction technique, in addition to its particular expressive qualities, enabled him to export his inventions outside Mantua. The contract signed in 1475 with Gian Marco Cavalli is explicit: the young goldsmith was obliged to keep his models and prints secret, under threat of severe penalties. For having done just this, Simone Ardizzoni, another engraver, was severely beaten on Mantegna's orders, and was to claim justice from the Marquis.

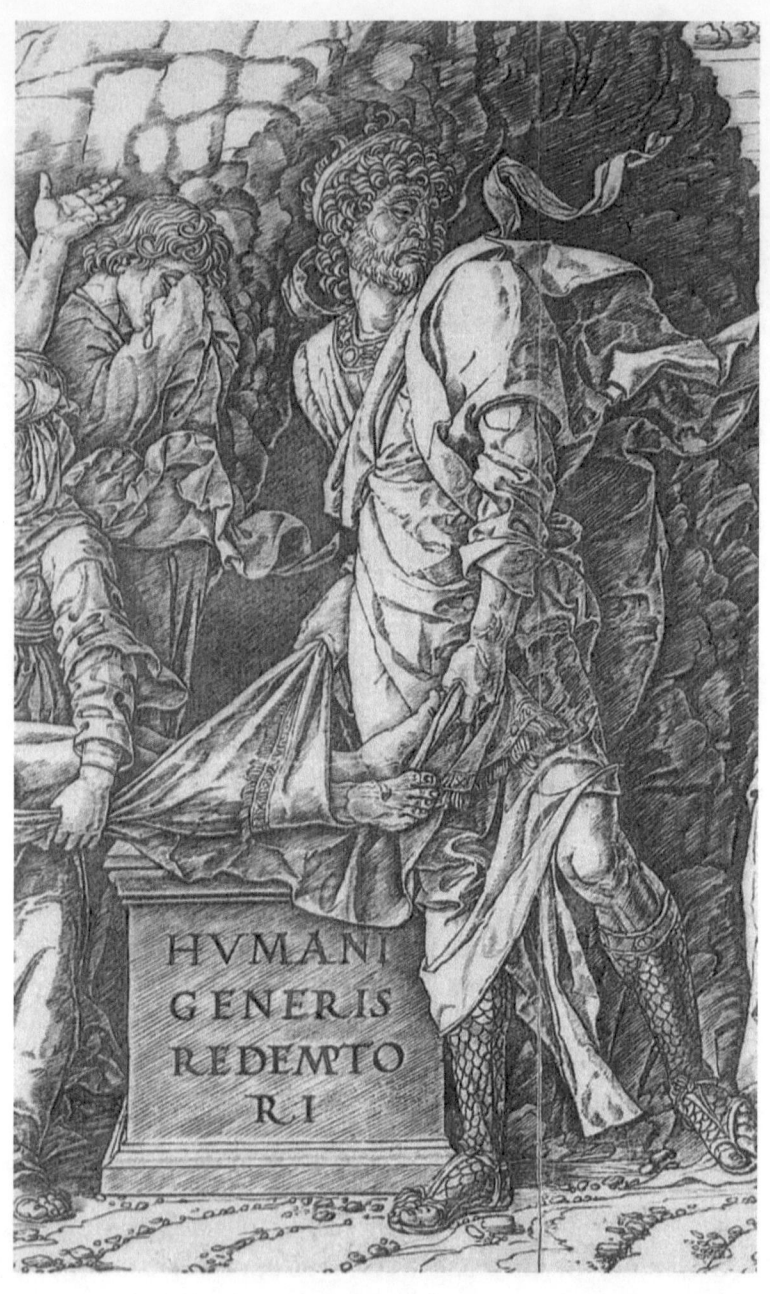

Detail

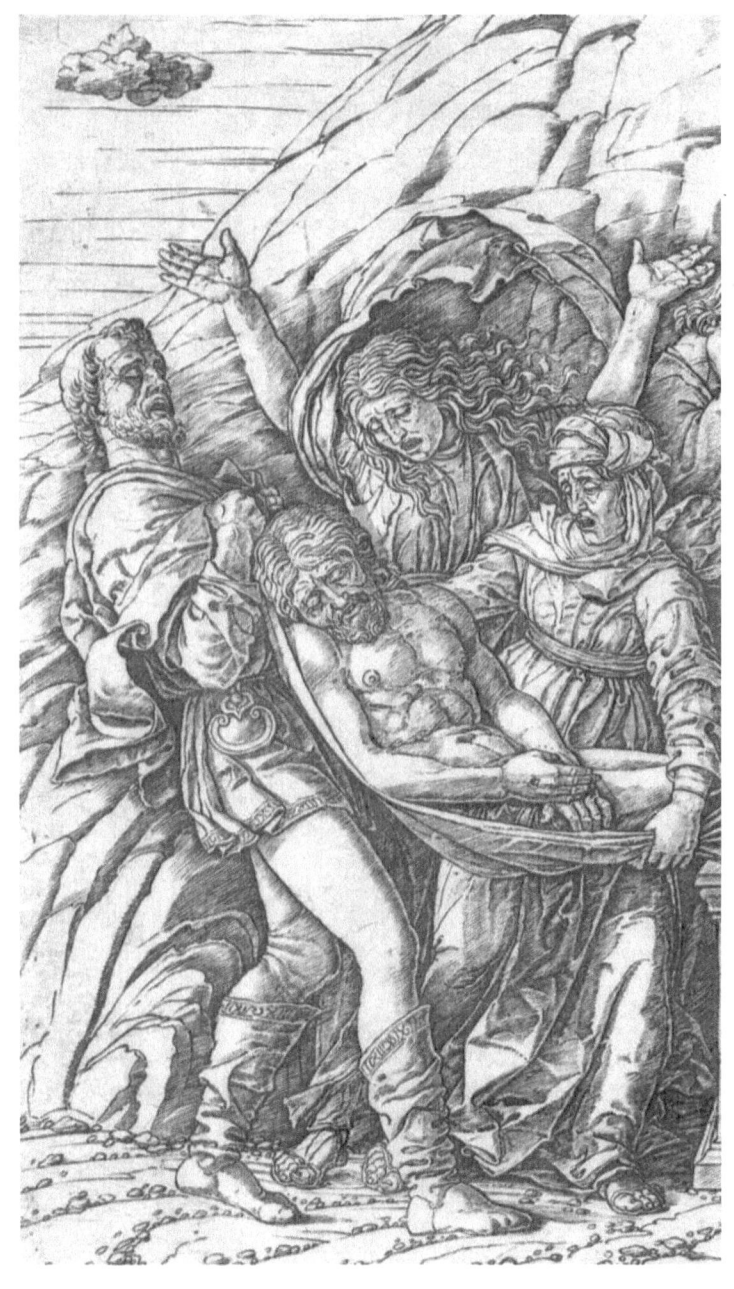

Detail

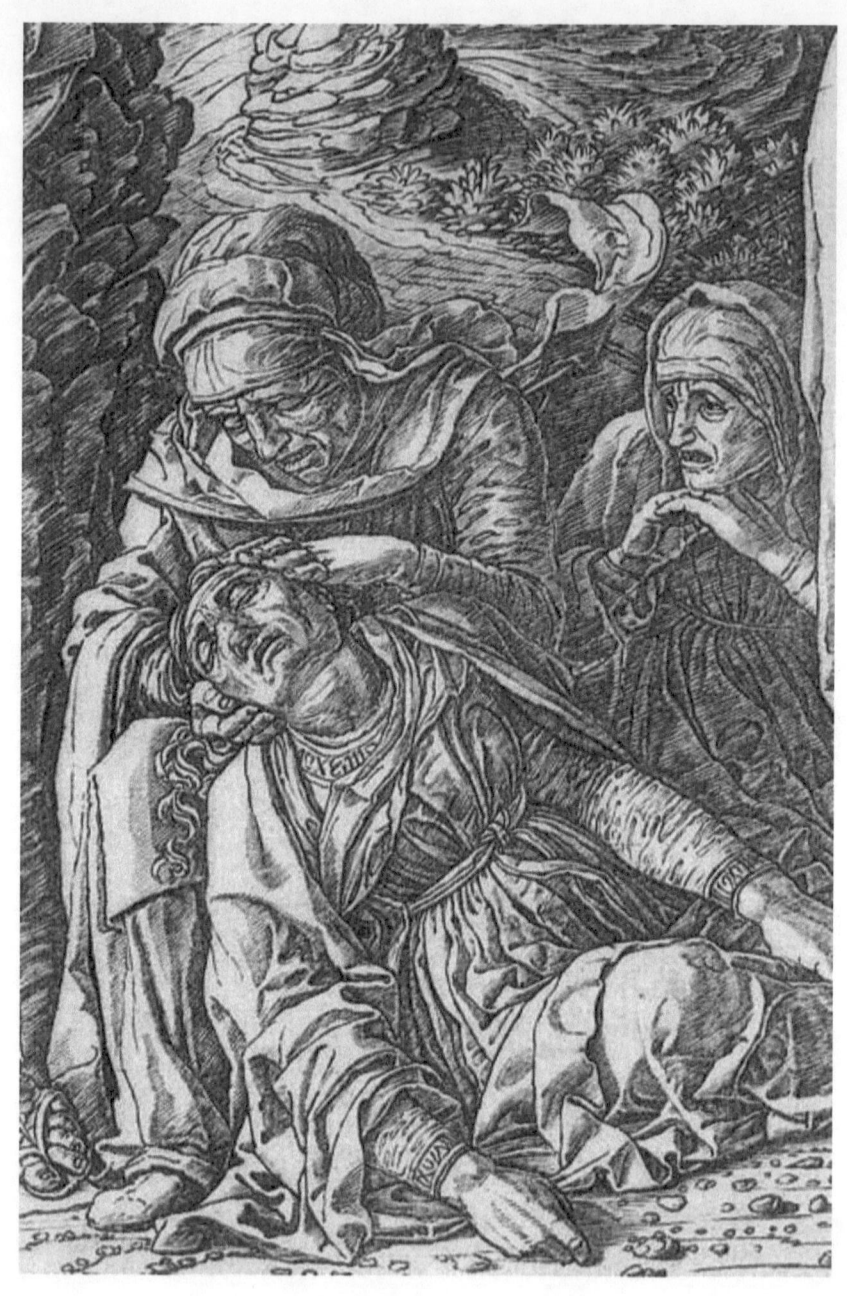

Detail

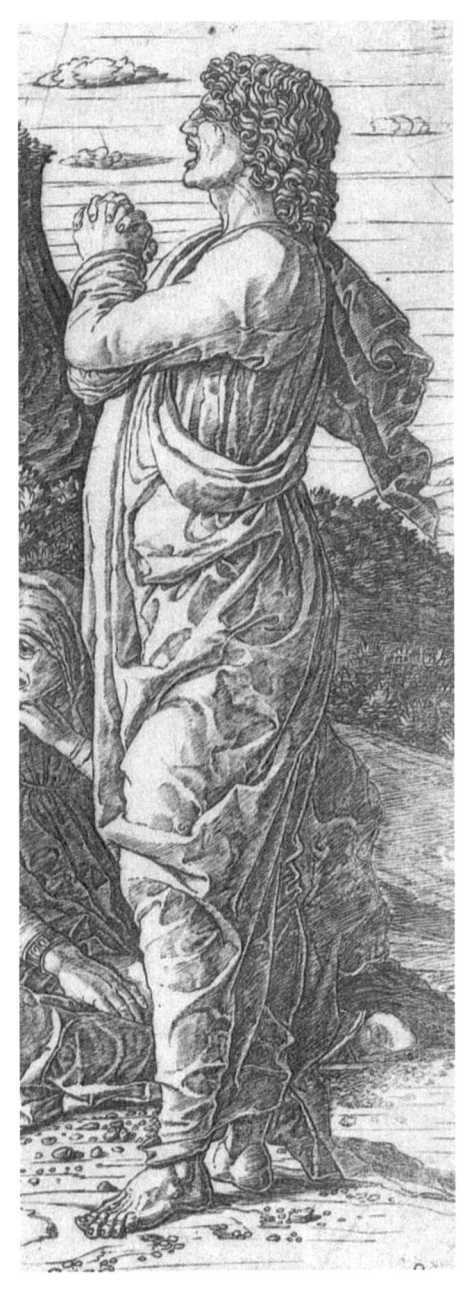

Detail

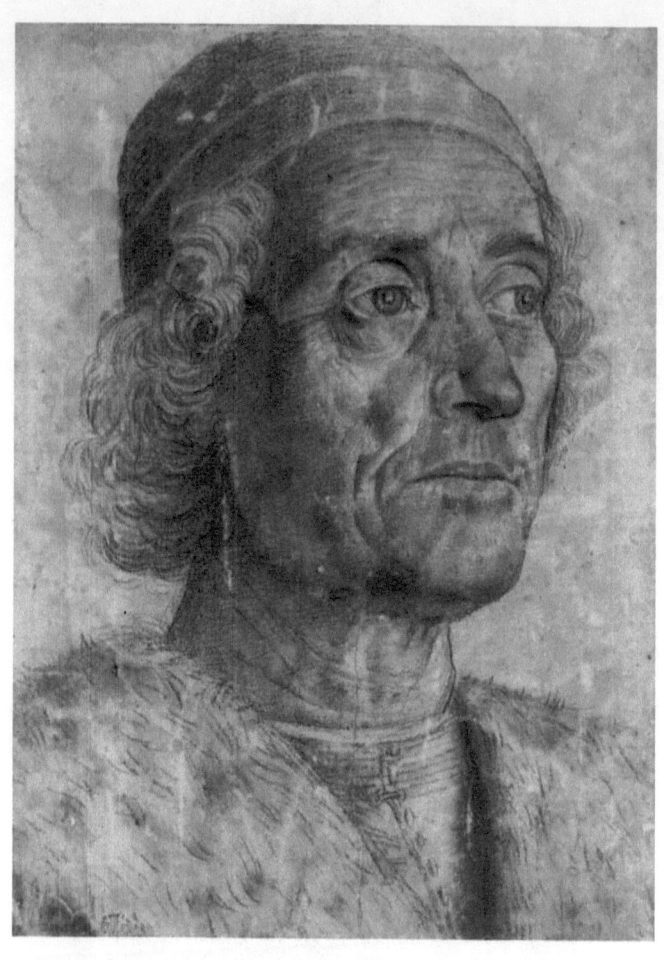

Portrait of a Man
1470-75, Black chalk on discoloured grayish brown
paper, 342 x 250 mm
This sheet is, even after much rubbing and
discolouration of the paper, among the most sculptural
drawn portraits of the fifteenth century. It is composed
with strong, animated strokes and bold shadows. It is
very close in character and style to several of the
frescoed portraits in the Camera degli Sposi.

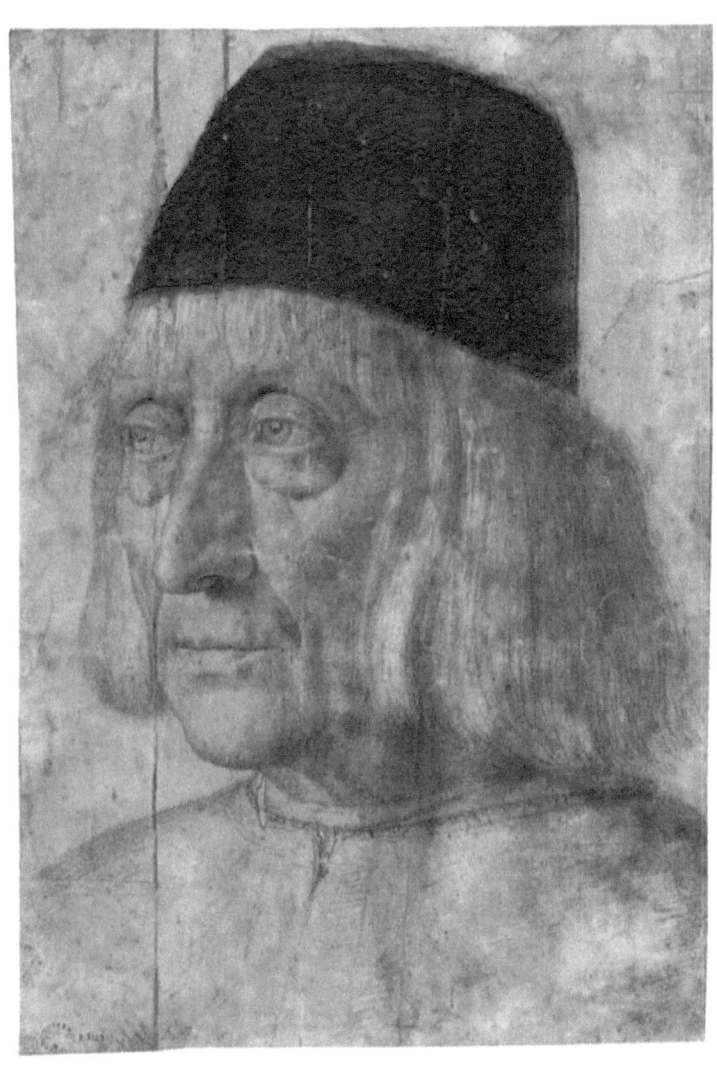

Portrait of a Man
1470-75, Black chalk on discoloured grayish brown
paper, 339 x 235 mm

The study of a man with black cap is entirely characteristic of Mantegna. (The cap was restored with gray-black wash.) The sheet is badly rubbed and has been reduced on all sides, but the sculptural and expressive resonance of the image is still present and deeply affecting. The technique, with lively parallel chalk strokes, is typical of Mantegna, as is the expressive clarity of both form and psychology.

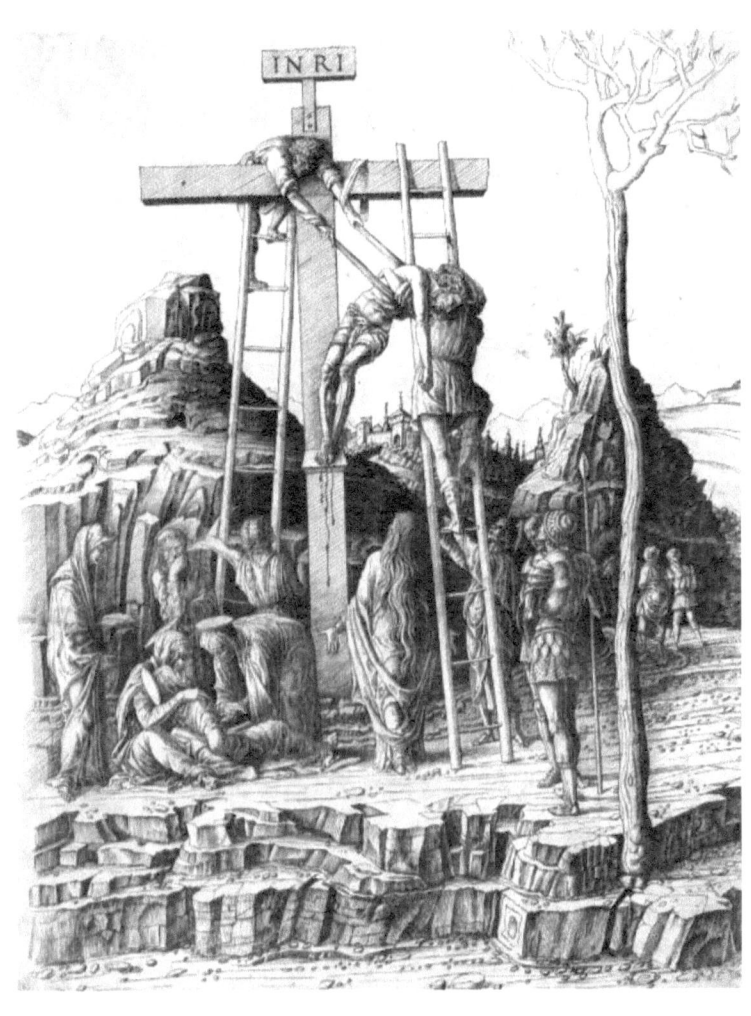

The Descent from the Cross, 1475, engraving

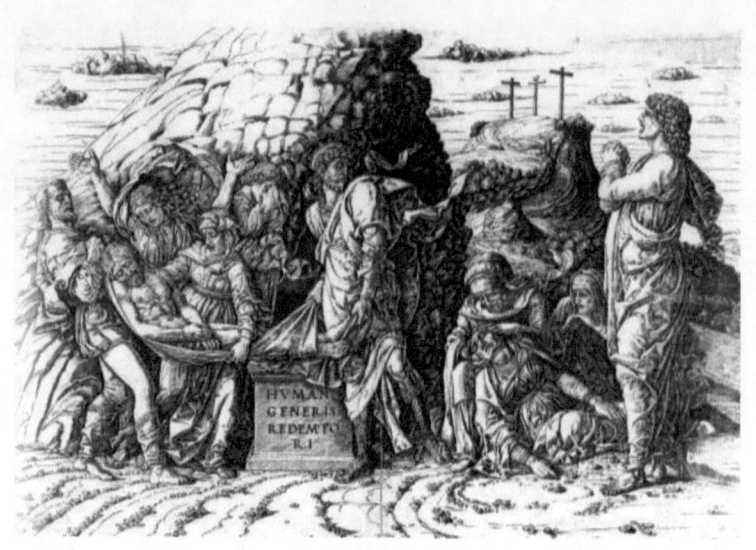

The Entombment, 1475, engraving

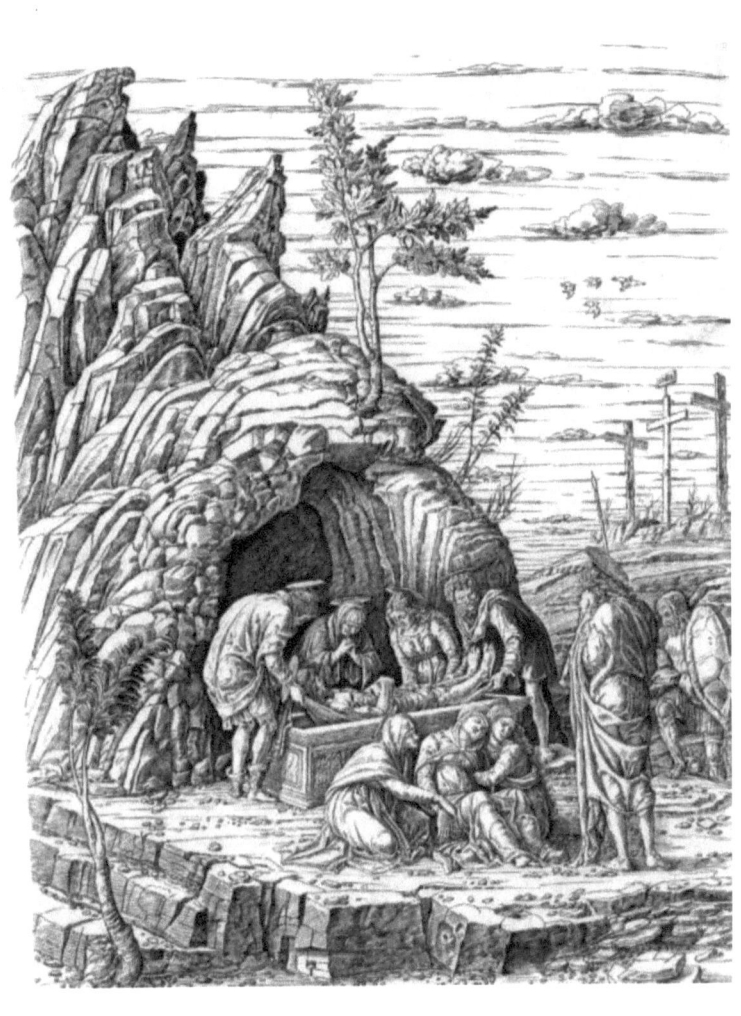

The Entombment, 1475, engraving

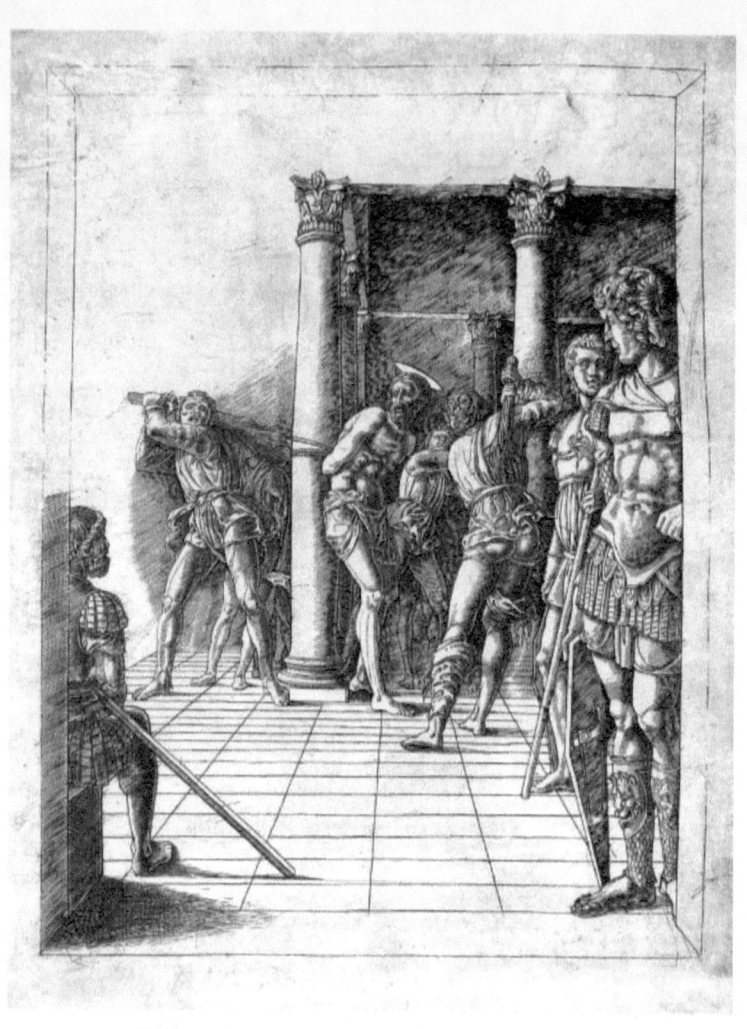

The Flagellation of Christ in the pavement, 1475, engraving

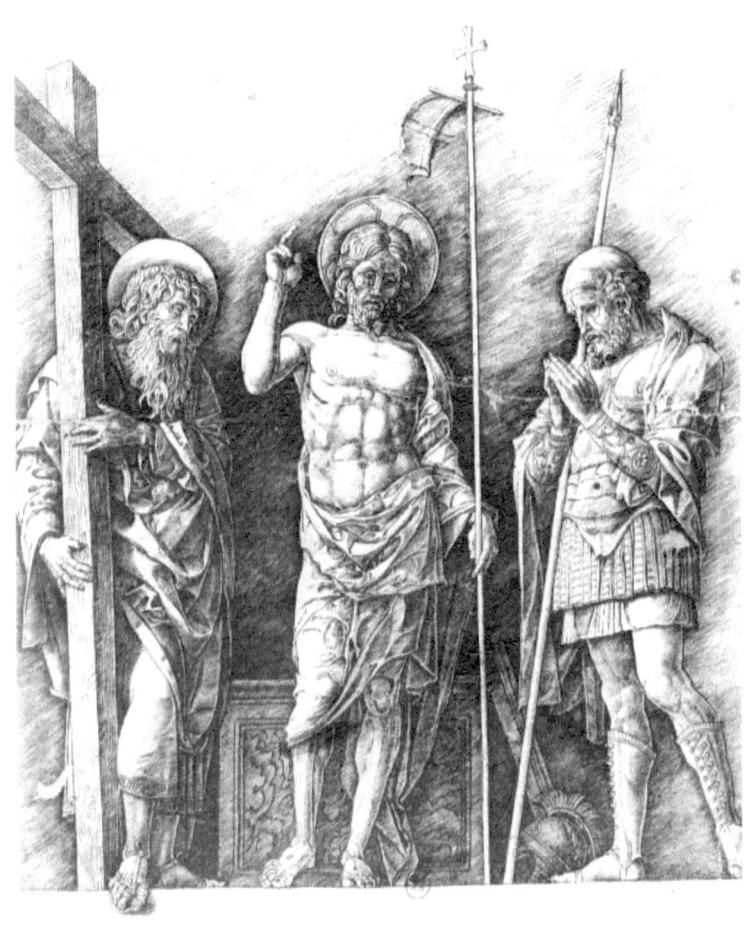

The resurrected Christ between St. Andrew and
Longinus, 1475, engraving

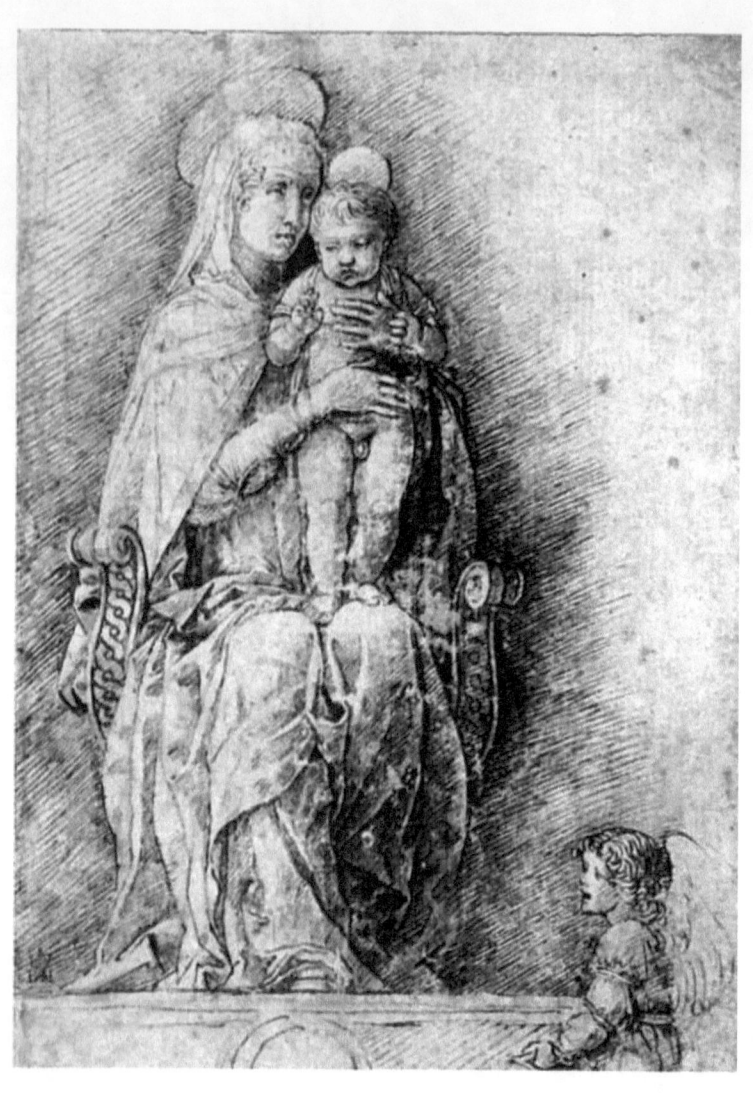

Virgin and Child, 1478,

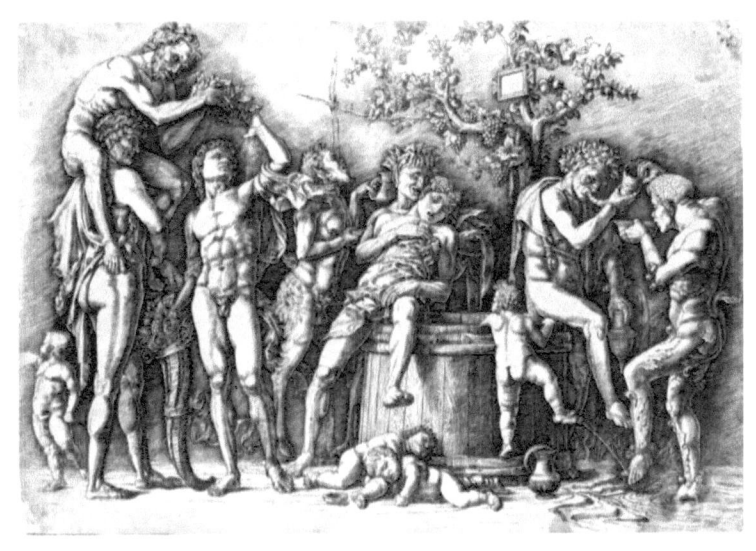

Bacchanalia with a Wine, 1480, Engraving

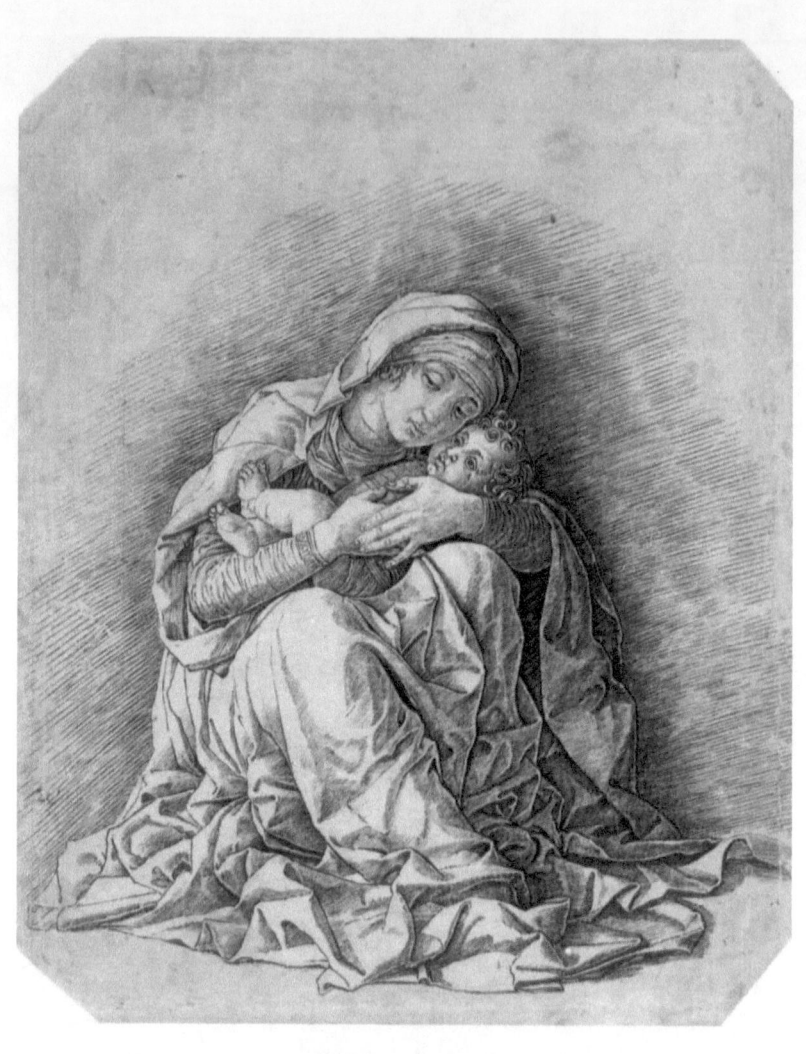

Virgin and Child
1480-85, Engraving, 262 x 233 mm

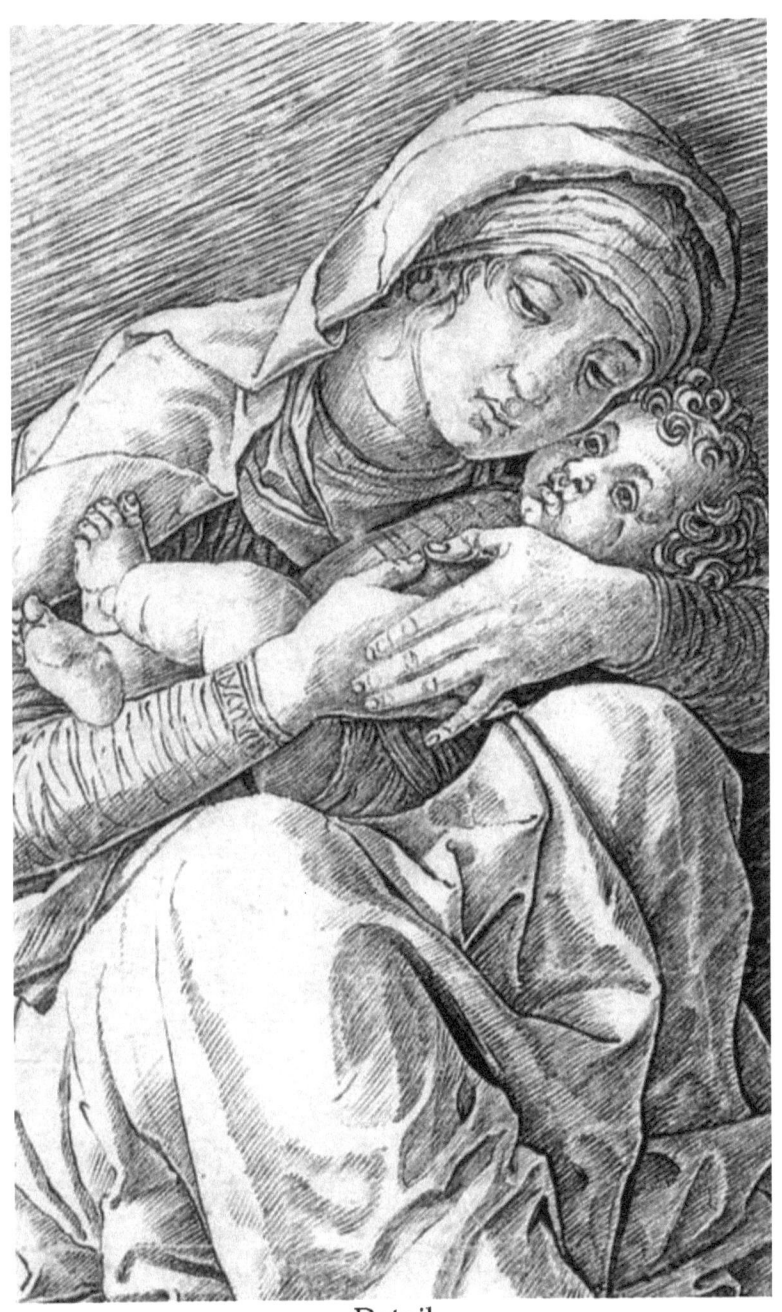

Detail

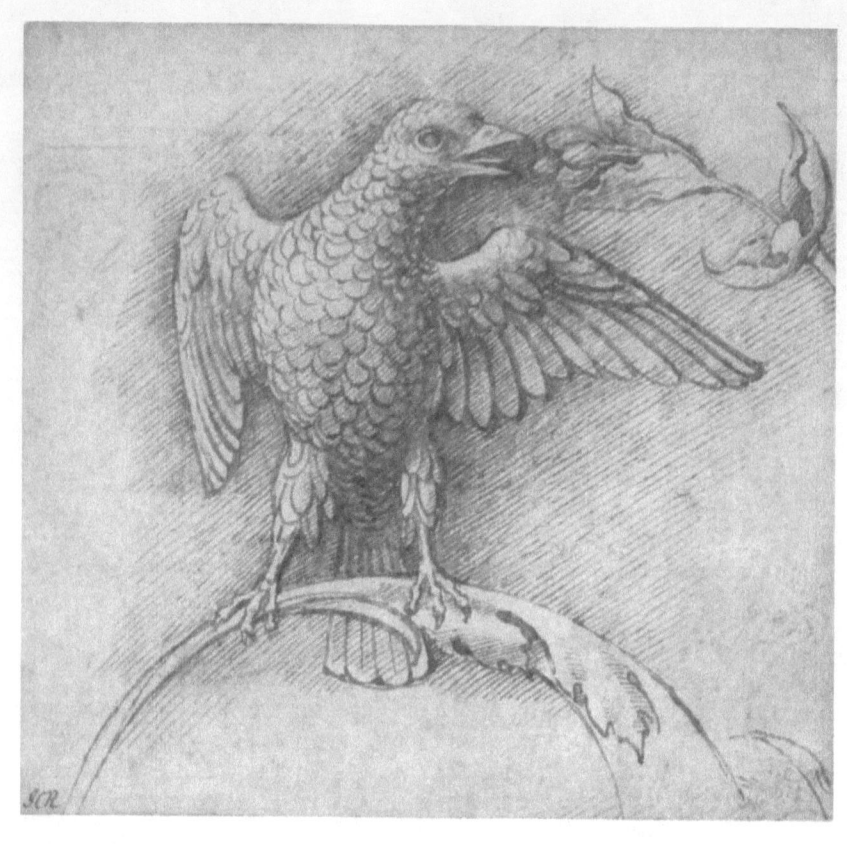

Bird on a branch
1485, engraving

.

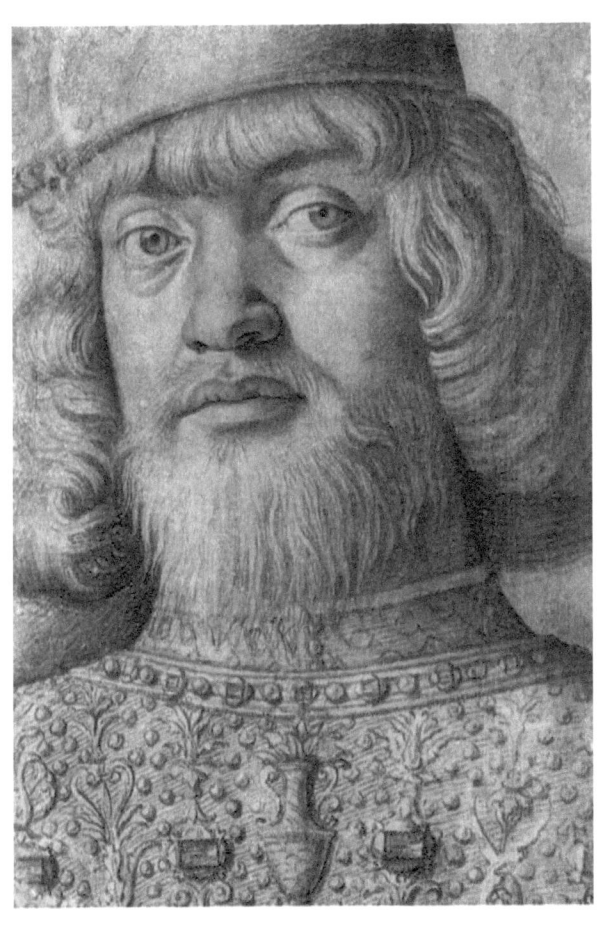

Francesco II Gonzaga
1490s, Black chalk, highlighting with brush, and white
gouach on greenish paper, 347 x 328 mm

This sheet has been reduced to the extent of having
virtually no space around the figure. Nevertheless, the
powerfully sculptural form projects from the sheet with
expressive animation. The commanding frontal
presentation of the sitter lends the portrait a dramatic
expressiveness unsurpassed in drawn portraiture.

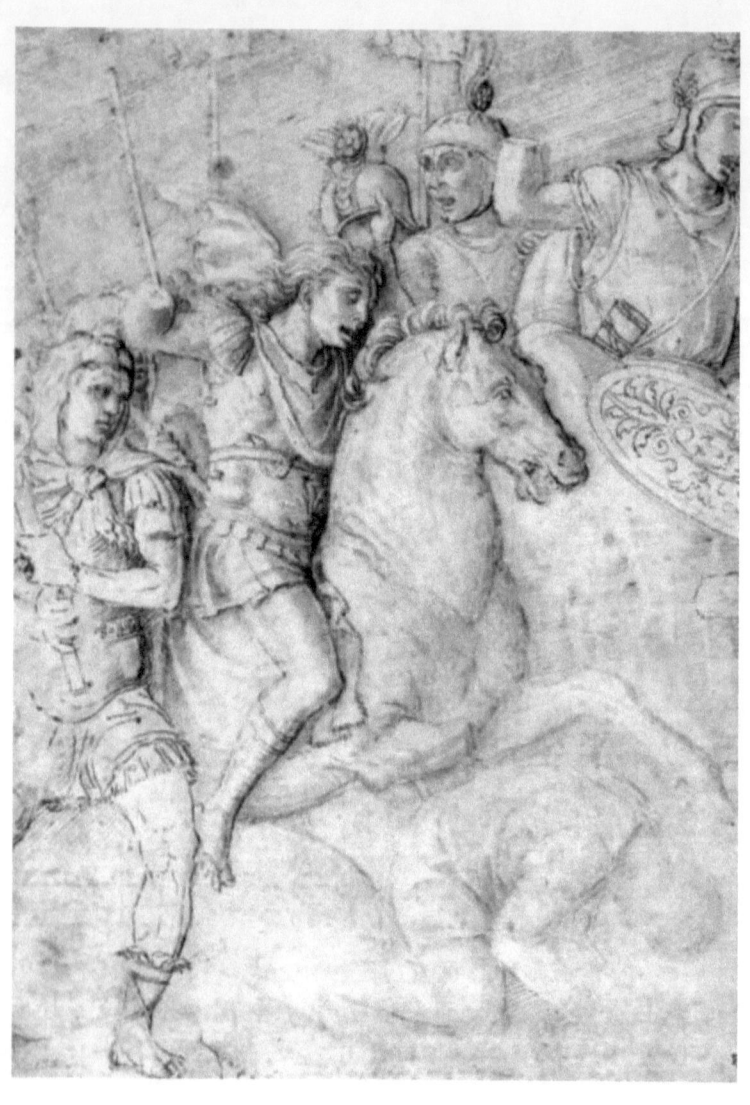

Study of an Ancient Bas Relief of the Arch of
Constantine, 1490, pen and ink

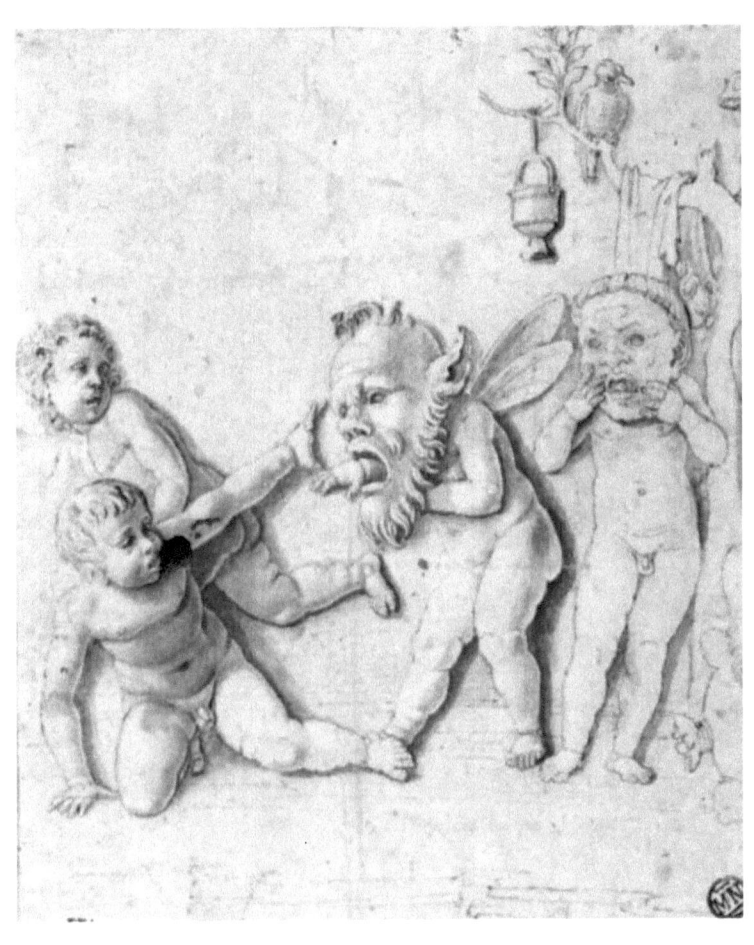

Children playing with masks, 1495

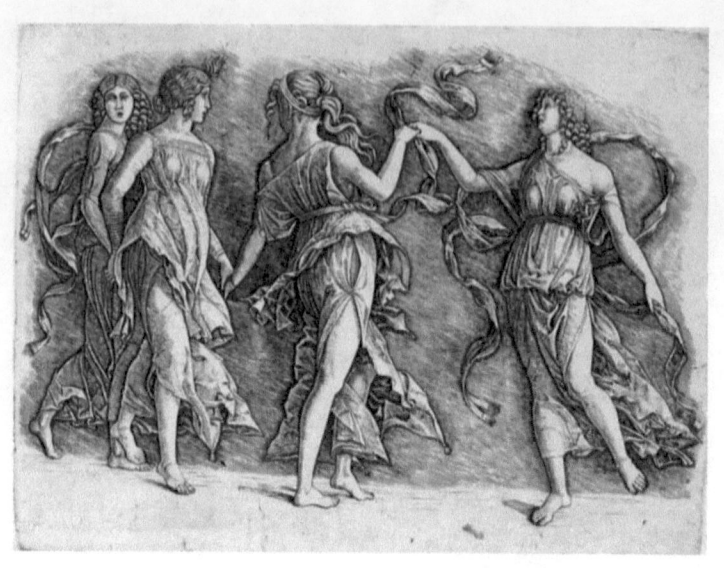

Four Muses, 1497

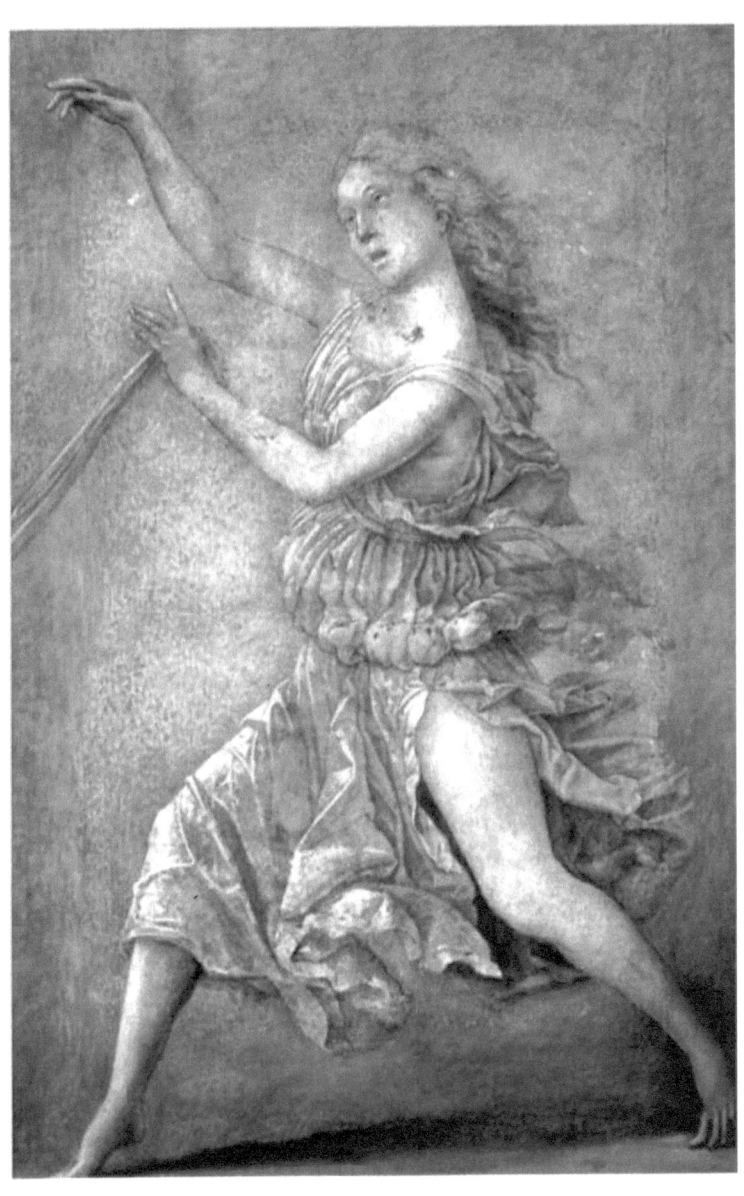

Muse, 1497

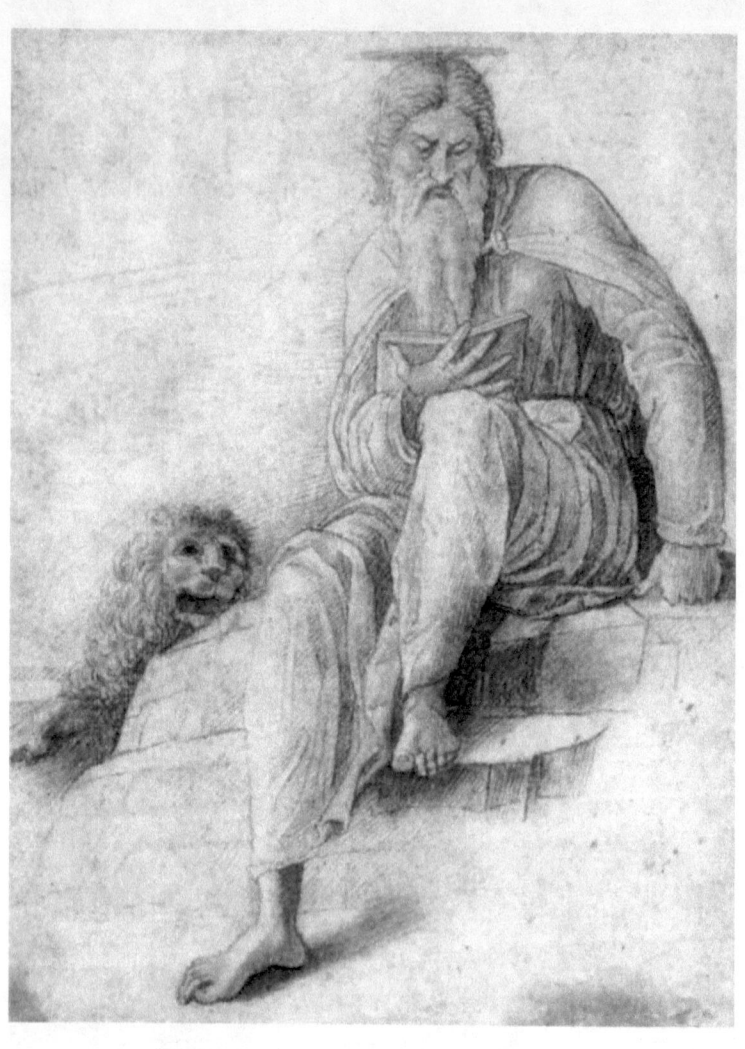

Saint Jerome reading with the Lion, 1500, chalk

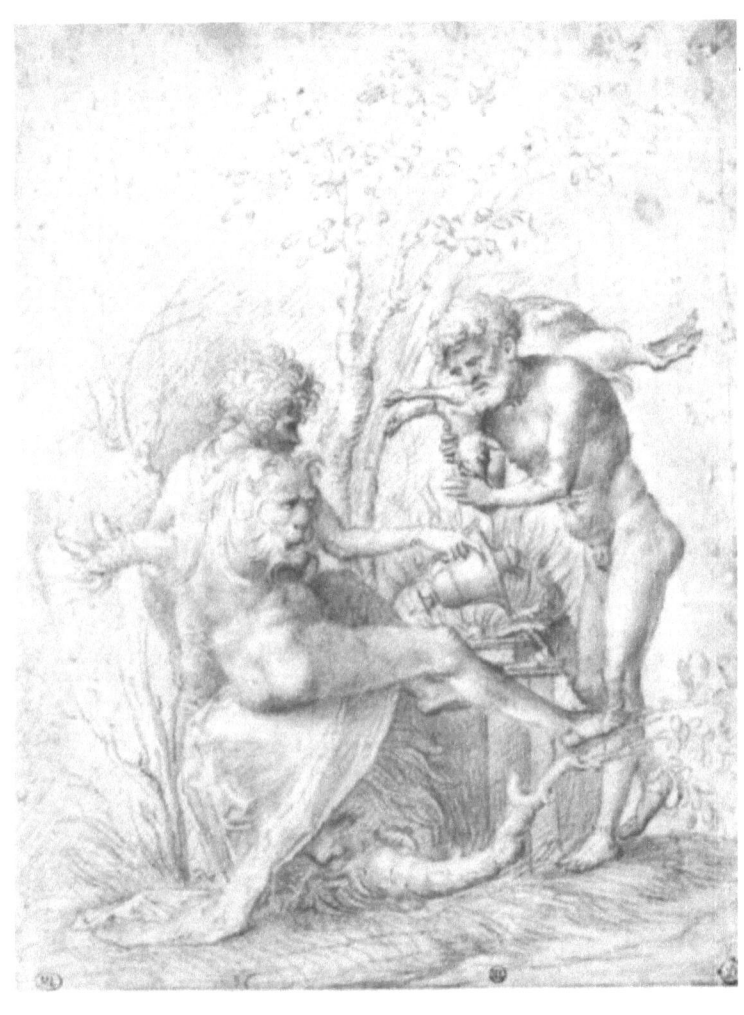

Molorchos making a sacrifice to Hercules, 1506

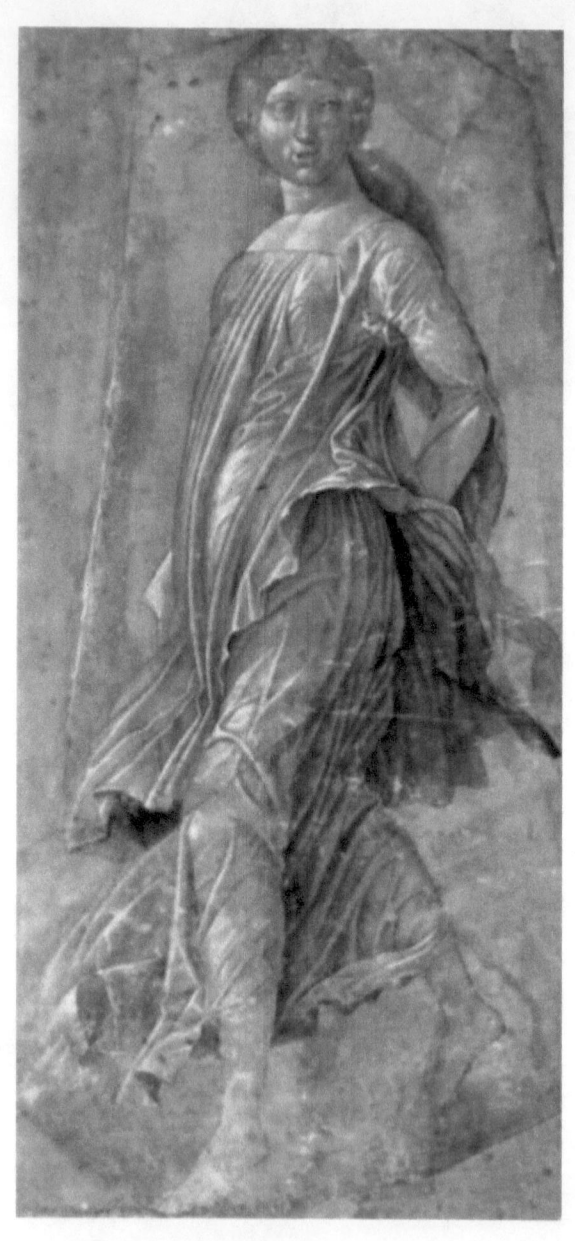

Muse

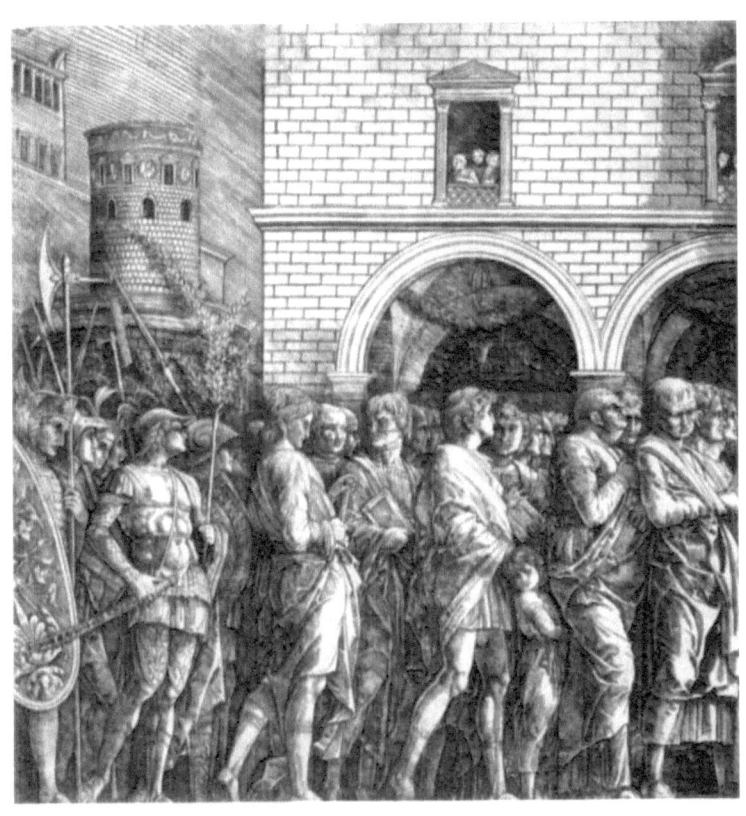

The Senators, engraving